Advance Praise for *Changeable*

"Reaching our full potential requires opening ourselves up to change—even when it's uncomfortable and scary, or seems impossible. The insights in this engaging book shed light on the real obstacles to change, and how we can overcome them—in ourselves and others. An empowering read."
　　—Susan David, PhD, bestselling author of *Emotional Agility*

"Changeable is a great book. Dr. Ablon addresses the most challenging aspect of human interaction—how to engage with another person to effectively help them change. This is the key task of a parent, coach, teacher, supervisor, therapist—just about any human-to-human interaction involves change. The clear and compelling way that Dr. Ablon outlines the Collaborative Problem Solving process will be a revelation. Using the principles outlined in *Changeable* will shift the way you understand and interact with others—and the impact may just change *your* life."
　　—Bruce D. Perry, MD, PhD, senior fellow,
　　　The ChildTrauma Academy, and bestselling author of
　　　The Boy Who Was Raised as a Dog

"Each of us has the potential to learn new skills, regardless of how we've been labeled or judged by others. In this empowering book, Stuart Ablon shows how helping others work past their struggles to learn and grow can yield powerful results."
　　—Scott Barry Kaufman, PhD, author of *Twice Exceptional*
　　　and *Ungifted*, and coauthor of *Wired to Create*

"We've trained thousands of our staff in states across the country to use the Collaborative Problem Solving model as a way to reach children with the most severe emotional and behavioral problems—children who were simply unreachable before. It's a clinical approach and parenting model, but we've also found the ideas and proven strategies of CPS can be applied anywhere there is a need to develop and grow people in a way that enhances skills. CPS has become an important staff development tool in addition to serving as one of our primary clinical approaches for helping thousands of children and families each year."

    —Patrick W. Lawler, CEO of Youth Villages

"Dr. Ablon has provided us with a clear and compelling roadmap of how to employ the Collaborative Problem Solving method, which will help parents, teachers, and clinicians to work with, not against, our children in crafting individualized strategies to encourage positive emotional and cognitive development while decreasing disruptive behavior. Thank you, Dr. Ablon, for this highly valuable contribution!"

    —Jess P. Shatkin, MD, MPH, professor of child and
       adolescent psychiatry and pediatrics, NYU School of
       Medicine, and author of *Born to Be Wild*

"Changeable is a hopeful, accessible, and essential book about the infinite power of human beings to change. I wish I could put this book in the hands of everyone who is struggling with how to help someone with their behavior."

    —Vanessa Diffenbaugh, author of *The Language of Flowers*

CHANGEABLE

HOW COLLABORATIVE PROBLEM SOLVING CHANGES LIVES AT HOME, AT SCHOOL, AND AT WORK

●

J. STUART ABLON, PHD

A TarcherPerigee Book

tarcherperigee

An imprint of Penguin Random House LLC
375 Hudson Street
New York, New York 10014

Most TarcherPerigee books are available at special quantity discounts for
bulk purchase for sales promotions, premiums, fund-raising, and educational needs.
Special books or book excerpts also can be created to fit specific needs.
For details, write: SpecialMarkets@penguinrandomhouse.com.

Library of Congress Cataloging-in-Publication Data
Names: Ablon, J. Stuart, author.
Title: Changeable : how collaborative problem solving
changes lives at home, at school, and at work /
J. Stuart Ablon, PhD.
Description: New York : TarcherPerigee, [2018] | Includes bibliographical
references and index.
Identifiers: LCCN 2017058351 (print) | LCCN 2017059929 (ebook) |
ISBN 9781101993132 | ISBN 9780143129011 (alk. paper)
Subjects: LCSH: Behavior modification. | Change (Psychology)
Classification: LCC BF637.B4 (ebook) | LCC BF637.B4 A25 2018 (print) |
DDC 153.8/5—dc23
LC record available at https://lccn.loc.gov/2017058351

Printed in the United States of America
1   3   5   7   9   10   8   6   4   2

Book design by Elke Sigal

To my pride and joy: Paige, Carter, and Jack

Author's Note

I have changed the names and other identifying details of many of the people represented in the stories in this book so as to protect their identities. The stories are real.

Contents

CONTENTS

Introduction

You're in a psychiatric hospital, face-to-face with a seriously ill patient who won't comply with the rules and who hasn't been taking his meds. His cheeks are turning red, his voice is rising—he's getting agitated. What do you do? This patient is delusional. He hears voices and thinks people are out to get him. He has a history of violence, having injured or killed people. He's physically bigger than you. How do you react?

Staff at the Oregon State Hospital in Salem, Oregon, face scenarios like this every day. The hospital is a massive thirteen-hundred-bed institution that houses some of Oregon's sickest, most violent patients, including many who have been deemed criminally insane. If you saw the movie adaptation of Ken Kesey's classic book *One Flew Over the Cuckoo's Nest*, then you know the Oregon State Hospital. The movie was filmed on its grounds, and some of its staff appeared as extras. Make no mistake, the Oregon State Hospital is every bit as intimidating as the film portrays it. To enter or exit, you traverse a series of checkpoints with locked steel doors. Cameras are everywhere. Even the bathrooms for visitors are high security. They are prison toilets, with nothing you can rip off or otherwise use as a weapon.

For years, staff at the Oregon State Hospital responded to challenging behavior by cracking down. Sometimes they had no choice but to physically restrain patients, burly staff members pouncing on them and putting them in choke holds. Other times they locked patients in padded seclusion rooms for hours, or they took away privileges, docking patients the points for good behavior that they needed to enjoy perks like movies or snacks.

If you think such measures produced a peaceful, harmonious, healing environment, you're wrong. Oregon State Hospital has a dark history of abuse of patients and of patient attacks against staff. A 2014 survey found that a quarter of the staff "had been physically assaulted by a patient in the past year," and "[o]nly 54 percent felt safe in their job."[1] Some unhappy staff members went so far as to post on Facebook pictures of gruesome wounds sustained at the hands of patients.

Hoping to improve conditions, staff on certain units embarked on a radical experiment, one that seemed foolhardy and even dangerous. They started being nicer. When challenging behavior arose, they didn't crack down. Instead, they approached patients and, in a calm and orderly fashion, tried to talk through the problem without imposing a solution. They also changed how they thought about challenging behavior. Rather than assuming that patients had willfully acted out and broken the rules, they chose to believe that patients would behave well if they could, and that they weren't behaving well because they weren't capable of it—they lacked various cognitive skills related to the solving of problems.

With this baseline of empathy, staff tried to investigate patients' points of view more deeply, understanding what underlying concerns had prompted their challenging behavior, while also articulating their own concerns. They hypothesized that the traditional punishments had probably sparked many violent outbursts in the past, provoking patients and causing their emotions to escalate. Dispensing with these punishments and engaging in dialogue, they hoped to resolve conflicts more peacefully, in ways that would satisfy patients and staff alike.

You can understand why this approach might have seemed "soft." Maybe talking it through would work with relatively healthy patients, but how could you conduct a calm, rational conversation with someone who is psychotic and potentially violent? What if the patient couldn't handle the conversation? What if he blew up? As one staff member at the hospital told me, "When you have a six-foot-four, 275-pound patient lose it . . . people have a real risk of being hurt."

It turns out that you *can* resolve conflicts with challenging people using so-called softer techniques. One middle-age patient whom I'll call Jim had a history of paranoid schizophrenia. He experienced frequent delusions, believing that the FBI was beaming thoughts into his brain, and that people around him could read his thoughts. Having gone off his medication, he was paranoid and refused to interact with others. He wouldn't attend therapy sessions at the hospital, complaining that staff and patients were reading his thoughts. He just didn't trust them, he said.

Instead of forcing Jim to comply, a nurse approached him to discuss his behavior. "Hey," the nurse said, "I've noticed you haven't been going in for treatment. I'm wondering why." Initially, the question prompted a superficial answer, but after three or four tries and a lot of reassurance, the nurse uncovered his concern: People could read his thoughts. "That sounds kind of scary," the nurse said, imagining how she would feel if everyone could hear her every thought. She then articulated her concern—the patient needed treatment if he was to get better. Instead of demanding that he comply with his treatment plan, she asked him how they might solve the problem so as to address *both* of their concerns. In truth, she was skeptical that talking the problem through would resolve the situation. But the patient had an idea: "What if I were to put tinfoil on my head?"

Huh?

In a way, it made sense. As the patient explained, other people read his mind through radio waves. But in his delusional state, he thought that a metallic substance like tinfoil blocked the waves. If he wore tinfoil over his head, nobody would be able to read his thoughts, and he'd feel safe.

The nurse wasn't sure about that solution. She thought the tinfoil might distract other patients in group therapy sessions. Yet again, the patient came up with a solution: He could put a thin layer of tinfoil over his head, and then mask it by wearing a baseball hat. None of the other patients would even know.

Although certainly unorthodox, the solution worked—for both of them. The patient was allowed to wear tinfoil under a baseball hat, and he willingly attended his therapy sessions. Problem solved. Potentially violent altercation avoided. Instead of inflicting more trauma on the patient by punishing him, the conversation engendered trust between him and the staff member. Jim and his nurse had worked out their difficulties *together*.

Through countless daily instances such as this one, individual units at Oregon State Hospital have begun to see improvements. Across all units where this approach has been introduced, the use of seclusions dropped by 34 percent per year and restraints by 40 percent. Injuries to patients and staff declined by 24 percent and 12 percent, respectively. On one unit, acts of aggression among patients plummeted more than 70 percent.[2] Staff members have described the change as palpable, observing that the hospital is transforming into a more humane and compassionate place. "It used to be cool to treat patients here like shit," one staff member told me, but it wasn't any longer. The new approach was "making it cool to be nice to patients." A patient related how much he liked the new approach as well, noting that "people in this unit really are actually trying to talk to me."

An Everyday Alternative to "Tough Love"

All of us encounter people in our daily lives who don't do what we'd like them to. Our kids act out, or our employees come in late to work. We have a dispute with a customer service representative on the phone, or with a friend, or with a spouse, or with a total stranger standing in line at the grocery store. In these situations, we can feel tempted to respond aggressively and assert our authority, even if we don't actually possess any. We might threaten the other person with a consequence. Or we might offer an incentive in exchange for compliance. Either way, we try to assert our will. Seldom do we take time to hear the other person out, to empathize with his or her concerns, and to work out a solution that leaves everyone satisfied.

Our institutions don't apply empathy very often, either. Discipline in America has long proceeded on the assumption that people behave in challenging ways on purpose. It follows that to make offenders want to behave well, we must take steps to reward good behavior and punish bad behavior. Our homes, schools, prisons, mental health facilities, and workplaces all operate according to the notion that we can motivate people to behave by manipulating them using rewards and punishments. In public life as well, it's common for politicians to play to people's fears, promising to crack down and get tough on criminals, terrorists, or other countries that hurt us or otherwise fail to meet our expectations, and to lavish rewards on individuals and groups that appear to serve the public good.

Rewards and punishments seem like common sense, but they are abysmal failures. We incarcerate more criminals than any other nation, hoping to deter future offenses, yet roughly three-quarters of inmates are rearrested within five years of their release.[3] Our schools fight challenging behavior through "zero tolerance" policies and punishments like time-outs, detentions, suspensions, and expulsions, yet research shows that zero tolerance policies make our schools less safe and hamper education for millions.[4] In our workplaces, punitive human resource policies fail to curb abusive behavior and even outright violence, costing billions in productivity losses and making life miserable for many employees.[5]

Although this failure seems mysterious at first glance, we actually know why rewards and punishments fail to address challenging behavior. As decades of research in the neurosciences have shown, people who misbehave don't do so on purpose out of a desire to act out, get attention, or achieve some other end. They misbehave because they struggle

People who misbehave don't do so on purpose.

with thinking skills required to meet expectations and resolve disputes. *It's the skill, not the will, that matters.* Just as individuals with learning disabilities struggle with cognitive skills in the areas of reading, writing, or math, some people have difficulty with critical thinking skills like flexibility, frustration tolerance, and problem solving. They have trouble managing emotions and resolving conflict, and this leads to all kinds of challenging behavior, including aggression and defiance. Traditional discipline compounds the problem, diminishing people's motivation to behave by leaving them feeling controlled, manipulated, and misunderstood.

Despite the overwhelming scientific consensus, conventional approaches to managing difficult or challenging behavior—defined broadly as any behavior we don't like, or a failure to behave in ways we *do* like—remain locked in place because institutions and individuals aren't aware of other options. Most staff members at Oregon State Hospital didn't *want* to physically restrain sick patients or put them into seclusion rooms. But as many have told me, they didn't see any other way to keep order and maintain safety in the facility. Countless teachers have told me that they send students to detention because they feel that if they don't, they'll lose control of their classrooms. If you're a parent and you put your kids in time-out or revoke a privilege to control their behavior, ask yourself: Why do I do it? Chances are it's because you want your kids to respect your rules and you don't know how else to respond.

There is another way. Over the past decade and a half, my colleagues and I have trained tens of thousands of people at schools, prisons, police departments, treatment facilities, and other organizations (including the Oregon State Hospital) in an approach to conflict resolution called Collaborative Problem Solving (CPS). An alternative to rewards and punishments, CPS is a mind-set that authority figures can have about offenders, as well as a structured process for interacting in real-life situations— what my colleagues and I call Plan B. Both CPS and Plan B got their start during the late 1990s, when my former colleague and supervisor Dr. Ross Greene began seeking alternatives to traditional rewards and punishments in his work with "explosive" children. I had received my PhD and was doing a fellowship at Massachusetts General Hospital and Harvard Medical School. As part of my clinical work with kids and their parents, I participated in a supervision group Dr. Greene was running for therapists working with explosive kids. Dr. Greene and I found that we both wanted to offer new, more concrete solutions to parents. The families I saw were at their wits' end, clueless about what to do about challenging behavior, and they begged me for practical strategies. What could they do differently that would improve their family life?

In Dr. Greene's 1998 book *The Explosive Child*, he conceptualized three possible approaches to challenging behavior (or as he called them then, "baskets").[6] Basket A was to respond by imposing your will on the child. You try to make the person do what you want, often by levying punishments or offering rewards. Basket C was the opposite: responding to conflict by giving the child what he or she wants. Basket B was a more ambiguous, "compromise" basket. Instead of you getting your way or the child getting his or her way, you meet in the middle and find a solution there, one that wouldn't antagonize a child with weak skills. As conventional discipline wasn't working for many kids, compromise seemed poised to yield better results for authority figures. By not imposing their will, authority figures would have a way to address problems that accounted for children's skills limitations.

Dr. Greene and I taught parents about these three options in each of our clinical practices, and we explored how to apply Basket B. Working together, we eventually realized that Basket B had limitations of its own. Compromise wasn't a great solution for many problems, and it often left one or both parties dissatisfied. Instead, you had to engage in a *problem-solving process* with the child. You had to sit down with her, hold a conversation, exchange views, listen, investigate possible solutions together, and agree together to embrace one of these solutions. It was precisely this collaborative process, a specific kind of dialogue between parent and child, that distinguished Basket B from the other two baskets.

We changed our terminology, speaking of "plans" instead of "baskets," and we reframed Plan B as a collaborative process rather than a simple compromise. But we still weren't satisfied with our understanding of Plan B. We wondered whether it was bigger than we first imagined. Perhaps it was a process that allowed not just for the solving of problems but for *the building of the underlying skills*. As research in neuroscience has shown, people don't build thinking skills by practicing them from 4:00 to 4:50 on Tuesday afternoons in the therapist's office. They develop them little by little by *practicing them in the actual situations that are creating difficulty*. Small, repetitive doses of "good stress" over a prolonged period are what create new neuronal pathways in the brain. You have to flex your mental muscles, so to speak, in order to hone them, which is exactly what practicing thinking skills in *real* situations allows us to do.[7]

By engaging in the hard work of tackling a problem with someone, children would practice dozens of skills relevant for the resolving of disputes. By having a chance to voice their concerns in the course of solving a problem, they would practice identifying, clarifying, and expressing them. As adults provided reassurance and listened to their concerns reflectively, children would practice calming down and regulating their emotions. By having a chance to hear the adult's concern, children would practice empathy and the ability to consider another person's perspective as well as to learn how their behavior impacts others. The process of collaborating to brainstorm, assess, and choose a solution would help children practice skills such as flexible thinking, solution generation, and the linking of actions to outcomes. Introduced as a regular means of problem solving, Plan B would facilitate brain development by giving those small, repetitive doses of good stress, creating new cognitive associations and new pathways in the brain.

That, at least, was our hypothesis. As we applied Plan B in our clinic, we began to see both reduced incidences of challenging behavior as well as improvement in children's underlying skills. Subsequent research has confirmed these results. CPS and Plan B have achieved stunning results with America's most difficult adults and kids, helping them work through daily conflicts, and in the process, practice and develop the cognitive skills they lack. CPS and Plan B help authority figures handle conflict more skillfully, too. When parents and teachers practice this approach with kids, they report improvements in their own relationships with spouses, colleagues, bosses, neighbors, and others. They become more empathic, more skilled at working toward mutually satisfactory solutions, and less inclined to dictate answers simply because they possess more power.

Since 2008, when Dr. Greene and I parted ways, my team has extended the application of CPS and Plan B beyond just working with explosive children to help both children and adults in all kinds of settings. We've further developed and refined the approach by collaborating with leading neurobiologists, among others, and we've researched *how* it works. We've also had the opportunity to train organizations and communities—including the educational and mental health staff from entire states and provinces—in the approach. Initially just an intriguing option helpful for certain populations of people, CPS and Plan B have blossomed into a proven, evidence-based approach that can help virtually anyone build skills and change their challenging behavior.

Improving any skill requires dedication, and, let's face it, our society doesn't provide many opportunities for us to sit down and practice hashing out solutions together with others. But imagine if it did. Imagine if more people shifted their mind-sets, like the staff at Oregon State Hospital. Imagine if instead of rushing to impose our will on disruptive individuals in our homes and workplaces, more of us did the harder work of empathizing with them, brainstorming new solutions with them, and giving them opportunities to practice their problem-solving skills. Imagine if schools and prisons started to focus on listening to offenders and working with them to resolve disputes. Imagine if police officers, judges, spouses, friends, neighbors—even entire countries—began turning first to collaborative conversations to work out conflict. What would society look like? What would our *lives* look like?

Changeable offers a new way of thinking about discipline, conflict, relationships, and problem solving, as well as scientifically validated tools for tackling conflict in your own life. The first chapter introduces the paradigm-shattering idea that people behave well if they *are able*, not simply if they want to. Chapter 2 provides scientific evidence that, in fact, skill, not will underlies behavior, and chapter 3 establishes that traditional disciplinary actions are doing more harm than good, saddling us with astronomical costs. Chapter 4 walks through the Plan B process in detail, while chapter 5 recounts how my colleagues and I have successfully applied the approach with parents and in institutional settings like schools, prisons, and psychiatric facilities. Chapters 6 and 7 show how to use Plan B and the broader CPS approach to help teams be more effective at work and to get along better with family and friends.

Smart, Not "Soft"

Traditionalists will contend that I'm too soft on bad behavior—that we must hold people accountable and apply tough love. I counter that engaging individuals to do the hard work of crafting new solutions *is* holding people accountable. It's much tougher for a person to practice skills through collaboration than to just accept a punishment. Working hard to solve a problem you have caused is the most meaningful way you can accept responsibility.

It's usually more effective, too. Incentivizing someone to do what you'd like creates extrinsic motivation for good behavior but fails to instill *intrinsic* motivation—the internal drive to do well. As bestselling author Daniel Pink and others have shown, compelling a person to behave in desirable ways by using punishments or rewards significantly *decreases* a person's internal motivation.[8] Overuse of rewards, for example, leads people to become much more interested in getting the rewards, but less interested in the very goal you want them to pursue. The way to foster internal drive in others is to give them a sense of mastery, control over their environment, and empathic connectedness. Traditional rewards and punishments don't foster any of those elements. You're *removing* a person's sense of power, autonomy, and control by imposing your will, and you're antagonizing the other person, thus eroding her feelings of connectedness with authority. You're certainly not nurturing empathy, because you haven't shown it yourself in the course of levying punishments or rewards.

CPS conforms well to recent research in psychology about how people improve their behavior and perform at their best. In her book *Mindset*,[9] Stanford psychologist Dr. Carol Dweck distinguished between a "fixed" mind-set, in which people attribute their performance to qualities inherent in them, and a "growth" mind-set, in which people regard their performance as due to skills they can change. As Dr. Dweck suggests, adopting a growth mind-set will more likely lead people to improve over time, as it keeps them more optimistic and hopeful about what they might achieve and thus more motivated to take action.

CPS's overarching philosophy of skill, not will corresponds closely to Dr. Dweck's growth mind-set. If you believe that proficiency in skills leads to better behavior, you'll believe that you can improve by working on the skills—there's nothing "inherent" about your performance. Conversely, rewards and punishments induce people to adopt a fixed mind-set. If a person tries and fails in the face of punishment and feels she just isn't able perform the task, she and those around her are liable to lose confidence and think of her as an inherently "bad" person. What CPS does is *operationalize* the growth mind-set, giving people a process by which they can actually practice and build skills. It's not enough to think of yourself as someone who can learn, grow, and change. You also need a clear framework for doing so. That's what CPS provides.

When it comes to performance, we also hear a lot these days about how important it is to have grit if you want to change your behavior and achieve positive goals. As Dr. Angela Duckworth, professor of psychology at the University of Pennsylvania, has argued,[10] talent doesn't drive success as much as grit, or passion and perseverance. Of course, you're more liable to be gritty if you possess a growth mind-set—these go hand in hand. Influenced by Dr. Duckworth's research, many schools have tried to help kids become grittier. The problem is how. As I visit schools, I encounter many teachers and administrators who love the concept of grit but struggle with nurturing it in kids. Here again, CPS has practical relevance. You can help people become more passionate and persistent in their growth efforts by focusing on their underlying skills. Persistence draws on many skills related to flexibility, frustration tolerance, and problem solving. Build the skills, and people become grittier. CPS helps people make positive changes in their lives by remedying what had quietly been holding them back—not a lack of effort, but a lack of skill.

If you want to motivate people to behave better because *they* want to, if you want them to believe that they are changeable, and if you want them to become tireless and persistent in pursuing change, read on to learn more about CPS. And the approach has other benefits as well. At Oregon State Hospital, CPS hasn't cured patients of psychosis, but it has allowed staff to ease the agitation the patients feel and help them feel respected and understood. Over time, the process of collaboration has also enabled these patients to learn and practice the critical thinking skills they lack. Even with the sickest patients and in an institution as challenging as the Oregon State Hospital, we can make progress if we recognize that it's a lack of skill that causes behavior problems, if we approach people with compassion and empathy, and if we work with them to change how they think.

I have yet to meet a person who, deep down, *wants* to be bad. We all do the best we can to handle what life throws at us, using the skills in our repertoire. So let's shift our mind-set about conflict, problem solving, and discipline. You can achieve healthier, more productive relationships with people in your life, reducing the stress that comes with constant conflict. You can help others build their problem-solving skills, even as

Let's shift our mind-set about conflict, problem solving, and discipline.

you build up your own. Together, we can improve conditions in our homes, workplaces, and schools, spreading civility and compassion. All by collaborating better to arrive at creative solutions. All by understanding that we often lack the skill, not the will, to behave well. We are all changeable. But it all starts with helping one another change how we think.

CHAPTER ONE

Skill, Not Will

As a clinical psychologist at Massachusetts General Hospital, I've treated a lot of challenging children and adults—pretty much every variety of dysfunction, disorder, and misbehavior. When it comes to children, some of my favorite to treat are what I call inflexible kids. These kids can be extremely bright and high functioning in many ways. They have an almost uncanny ability to learn and memorize new information—it just seems to burn into their brains. But information retention is also the root cause of their difficulty. Because the cognitive associations they form are so strong, they can't be altered very easily. Once these kids experience something, that's it: A template forms, and they have a hard time adapting to even slight deviations. The inflexible kids I see glom on to structure, routine, and predictability. They must go to *their* restaurant, dress the way *they're* used to, sit in class where they've *always* sat. When life doesn't happen as they expect, they can't handle it. I call them "need to know" kids, as opposed to "go with the flow" kids. They perceive the world as black or white, good or bad, their way or no way, and nothing in between.

One inflexible kid I treated, eleven-year-old Susan, was an all-American girl who loved to play hockey and sent me pictures of her team every season. Susan's parents described her as strong willed, capable, and very intelligent, a great kid in most respects. She'd never had serious behavioral problems before. As Susan's mother told me, "About 85 percent of the time, she's a rock star. She's queen of the monkey bars, a strong swimmer and skier, a great gymnast, and a great hockey player." During the other 15 percent, Susan fell into fits of anger. "It's like a switch gets flicked," her father told me. "She'll yell at her sister or hit her. Does the same with her mom. She'll scream, 'I hate you; you're not the boss of me! You can't make me! Don't look at me! Don't touch me!'"

As bad as these tantrums might sound, in the world of challenging behavior, they're pretty minor. Susan wasn't violent. She didn't harm herself or others. She was coping well enough at school. Frankly, she didn't seem that hard of a case.

For the first several weeks of working together, we made progress in helping her parents understand how she was wired and how this wiring led to some of her challenging behavior. Susan seemed to enjoy coming to our sessions, and we forged a strong therapeutic relationship. It helped that her parents loved her and were bent on doing whatever it took to help their daughter.

Then on Susan's first day of middle school, her parents called and said they needed to see me—Susan was in crisis. I was able to fit her in that day, right after lunch. But that wasn't soon enough.

I was out grabbing a bite when I received a frantic text from my office: "Your one p.m. appointment is here. They need you!"

I ran back to the office to find Susan in hysterics. Her father was physically restraining her, and her mother was holding her shoes. As her mother told me, she had taken them so that Susan wouldn't launch herself through a plate-glass door and run away. "Susan, what happened?" I asked. She refused to speak to me. This was unlike her. We had developed such a solid relationship.

It took a good twenty minutes, but we managed to calm her using techniques I'll describe later in this book for dealing with people in crisis. Susan still wouldn't speak, but she would write words and phrases down on pieces of paper. Meanwhile, her parents relayed what had happened. Susan didn't want to go to school, and her parents had been trying to force her. Even her beloved grandfather couldn't manage to coax her into going. She had run away, and when she was brought back home, she said she wanted to kill herself. This was entirely out of character. She might have always had minor anger issues, but she never exhibited any explosive or suicidal behavior before. What could *possibly* be going on here?

It turned out that at overnight camp a few weeks earlier, Susan had suffered severe migraines and wasn't able to reach her parents by phone. The experience traumatized her. Now, as Susan confirmed through the phrases she was writing, she didn't want to go to school because she was deathly afraid she would get another migraine and not know whom to go to or what to do. She feared she would freak out as she had at camp, and the other students would stare at her and think something was wrong with her.

When I uncovered these concerns, they made perfect sense. As her parents and I had discovered, Susan struggled with cognitive skills related to flexibility. She needed more routine, planning, and predictability than other kids, and when these elements were lacking, she ran into trouble. Like other inflexible kids, Susan especially struggled with transitional situations in which existing templates didn't apply and she was forced to adapt to new conditions. Attending middle school for the first time was such a situation, and it made sense that Susan would have trouble with it. Everything in middle school was different from what Susan was used to: the kids, the lockers, the schedule, the teachers, the building itself—everything. If she got a migraine, she wouldn't know what to do. She had no template, no plan to follow. Susan got so upset and anxious that she didn't know how to express her feelings to her parents. All she could do was lash out. And her parents, who would otherwise have jumped to help her, didn't know what to do.

For many years, Susan's parents had interpreted her temper tantrums as a technique she used to get her way. Most parents would probably have come to a similar conclusion. Like Susan's parents, they would have dealt with Susan's behavior by punishing her, setting boundaries, and "teaching her a lesson." But in this instance, Susan clearly wasn't being difficult because she *wanted* to be. Her anxieties about a brand-new school and the possibility of getting a migraine there tied into her cognitive makeup, and the more her family tried to force her to go to school, the more explosive she became. Her well-intentioned parents were trying to force their inflexible child to do something she wasn't capable of doing. And that inflexible child, lacking the cognitive skills to deal with the situation and come up with a solution, did the only thing she could. She acted out.

Get Out of Line, Do the Time

Our society has an entrenched way of thinking about behavior. We almost always assume it derives from a person's *will*—that people behave consciously and purposefully. When people misbehave, we likewise assume that they're doing it intentionally. As a result, whenever individuals in almost any social setting act out or misbehave, those in charge usually respond by punishing the bad behavior. When you were a kid, did your parents take away your TV time or allowance when you misbehaved? Most did. When you continued to misbehave, they probably just stepped up the intensity of the consequences and rewards. And they probably also bestowed privileges when you did the right thing.

School discipline is similar. We assume that when kids misbehave in school, they do it on purpose either to get stuff (special attention, for instance) or get out of stuff (like doing their work or coming inside after recess). In the early school years, teachers punish kids with time-outs. They are taught that kids will use the time away from their peers to reflect on what they did wrong, and that they will feel badly enough at missing out and having been punished that they will want to behave better next time. As kids grow older, schools hand out detentions and suspensions that likewise isolate the offenders and are supposed to teach them a lesson. Statistically, these are the most common punishments in

U.S. schools,[1] and I should add that they are also levied dispro-portionately on kids with disabilities and those of color.[2] All along in our educational system, we assume that people mis-behave deliberately, and that reforming behavior means simply providing the right motivation.

When kids *really* act out and become uncontrollable, we remove them from mainstream schools and put them into thera-peutic schools or treatment centers, and, eventually, juvenile de-tention facilities. Later, we lock them away in adult prisons (I'll have more to say about this progression, which has been called the "school-to-prison pipeline"). These institutions also usually op-erate according to principles of punishment and reward. In some states, the law mandates very specific punishments for offenses by inmates at detention centers. In some facilities where I have worked, for instance, lying to staff, arguing when given instruc-tions, or disrespecting others can result in punishments like loss of privileges, early bedtimes, time-outs, and extra work assign-ments. Staff can reward good behavior by bestowing extra privi-leges such as more TV time, more time playing sports, and later bedtimes. Serious offenses, like possessing weapons or threatening staff, can prompt more serious punishments, like placement in a restricted program or even transfer to a different facility.

The treatment patients receive at most psychiatric hospitals is similarly organized. Virtually all psychiatric hospital care in the United States takes place within structured systems of disci-pline called point and level systems, token economy systems, or contingency management systems.[3] The institution marks progress in treatment by defining different levels that patients can attain. Behave well, and you bump up to higher levels, receiving more privileges (TV time, movies, special meals, home visits, and so on). When you sustain the highest level long enough, the institution will discharge you. But if you behave poorly, you slide down to lower levels, losing privileges. We assume that this carrot-and-stick approach will motivate people with psychiatric illnesses to behave better. Implicit in this assumption is that they've lacked the willpower in the past to behave well. People misbehave, we think, because they *want* to.

These practices, however, aren't reserved for people with serious emotional and behavioral disorders. Companies, governments, and entire countries deploy this approach to discipline in an attempt to shape behavior. Did you land a big client or make your numbers? Your boss may give you a bonus or promote you. Did you fail to follow protocol or get another unsatisfactory performance review? Your boss may place you on probation, demote you, or even fire you. Governments try to encourage "good" behavior (like going to college or saving for retirement) by offering rewards such as tax incentives. They discourage "bad" behavior (like polluting or violating workplace regulations) by levying higher taxes, slapping on fines, or providing for civil lawsuits. In foreign policy, we place sanctions on countries that flout international law, and we reward countries for good behavior by lifting sanctions, giving them privileged trading arrangements, and offering their leaders photo-op meetings with our president.

We persist in assuming that if we institute proper consequences, teaching offenders the benefits of behaving well and the costs of misbehaving, they will make better choices and mend their ways. We can trace this thinking back to the Bible and the vengeful God in the five books of Moses who levies harsh punishments onto the Children of Israel for their misdeeds. More recently, twentieth-century behavioral science has seemed to confirm the wisdom of punishments and rewards. Experimenting with rats, researchers found that by manipulating rewards and punishments they could encourage or discourage simple behavior.[4] Like rats, human behavior is an age-old matter of conscious choice and free will—nothing more. Or so it might seem.

Learning from a "Bad" Kid

But what if this thinking is wrong? What if people *don't* misbehave because they want to, but because they lack the skills to behave otherwise? As we'll see in the next chapter, a large body of neuropsychological research has disproved the notion that poor behavior is a choice, and it has affirmed the idea that skill determines good behavior. In fact, research in the neurosciences has identified *dozens* of specific, underlying skills that if absent or diminished result in challenging or "bad" behavior.

As compelling as this research is, you don't need science to understand it's the skill, not the will that matters. During my senior year in high school, when I first became interested in psychology, I got a job at a hospital psychiatric unit for kids. This locked facility admitted kids for short-term stints when they threatened to harm themselves or others. I was supposed to hang around and observe at first, but the unit was grossly understaffed. Almost immediately, staff asked me to help take care of patients in ways I never expected and, frankly, was not trained for.

During my first week, staff members and I were supervising

patients on the playground when a twelve-year-old boy—I'll call him Jason—had an explosive outburst. I ran over to lend a hand as the other staff members tried to calm him. Jason broke free and did the unthinkable: He kicked me and spit right into my face. One of the staffers, who was serving as my mentor at the facility, saw this happen. "Hold on," he said. "Let me teach you a few things about what to do here."

He grabbed Jason, turned him around, and showed me how to restrain him. He placed his arms around Jason's body, forming them into a kind of straitjacket. Meanwhile, he stood between Jason's legs so that the kid could not kick him backward.

Jason's outburst and the violence of the restraint unnerved me. But I was in for much more. A few hours later, Jason exploded again and was restrained. Jason was really out of control, so staff members forced him into a seclusion room and placed him facedown on a cold floor. One of the staff members sat on his back to hold him down, and they motioned for me to hold his legs. I did so for several minutes, and it wasn't pleasant. Jason was screaming, crying, writhing, spitting, and calling me and my mother all sorts of names.

Soon Jason ran out of energy and fell asleep on the floor. We, too, were drained. And I found myself struggling with competing feelings. I felt uncomfortable and ashamed to be helping— it seemed crude to me, inappropriate, wrong, as if I were inflicting still more suffering. Yet I felt empowered to be able to help with something so critical. I didn't say anything to the other staff about my ambivalence. They were the experts, and I figured that as painful as it was, restraining Jason was probably necessary or helpful. We were just doing what needed to be done.

That evening during my forty-minute drive home, I found myself feeling worse about my day. What had we been doing? Could restraining this poor kid really have helped him? Didn't I remember hearing in rounds about his history of physical and sexual assault at the hands of more powerful adults? Wasn't there another way?

The next morning, I put these misgivings aside and showed up for work. I was walking down a hallway, passing the quiet room, when I saw Jason in there. When he saw me, he swore at me. I didn't react, much as I wanted to. I just went on my way. Several hours later, I saw him yet again and braced myself, thinking he was going to spew more obscenities. To my surprise, he approached me with a forlorn look on his face. "Hey, sorry about what I said earlier. I didn't mean it. I just get kind of crazy sometimes. I'm not sure why."

I was stunned. Even today as I think about this story, I get goose bumps. In that moment, I understood the tragedy that Jason was living, and that all of us around him in positions of authority were enabling. Jason was saying awful things to me and others, repelling us and making us feel terrible. As a result, none of us wanted to be within ten feet of him. Yet Jason couldn't help it. He was out of control. He didn't know what to do about it. All he could do was apologize later. Ironically, the person who was probably *most* motivated not to suffer through another traumatic episode was Jason himself.

I couldn't imagine what Jason was feeling, how awful it must have been to go through life alienating everyone around you, without wanting to or understanding your own behavior. It was my first inkling that our traditional perspectives about why people misbehave were wrong—that people change if they are able, not if they want to, and that we need to consider this when trying to help them. The staff at this facility could "correct" Jason's behavior all they wanted with restraints, seclusions, and other punishments, but it wouldn't help. Thanks to a lack of skills, Jason was stuck in a cycle of bad behavior, and the institution was stuck, not knowing what to do. Staff do the best they can, too— and so do institutions like this one. We're all trying the best we can to handle what life is throwing at us with the skills and information we have at our disposal. If we have only traditional rewards and punishments at our disposal to help address challenging behavior, we usually come up short.

The *Real* Reason People Don't Do What We Want

To help parents free themselves of conventional thinking and appreciate the wisdom of *skill, not will*, I often ask them to consider more closely the situation in which a kid refuses to do his homework. Why does the kid refuse? Parents will say, "It's obvious—he doesn't *want* to!" But that logic implies that the kids who *are* doing their homework do so because they want to do it. Really? Do you know any kids who are excited to do their homework when they could do something else, like play video games or text their friends? Trust me, it's the rare kid who wants to do his homework. Most kids don't want to do it but do it anyway, and some who don't want to do it, don't. The reason this second group of kids don't do their homework is because they lack skills of one sort or another—skills that are necessary in

RETHINKING "GOOD" BEHAVIOR

During the past twenty-four hours, did you do something that you found unpleasant or uncomfortable, like get up for work early or endure an hour in heavy traffic to pick up your kids from practices or rehearsals? Why did you do it? Clearly you didn't want to get up at 4:30 a.m. or drive at a crawl down a stretch of highway. What motivated you? Was it someone dangling a reward before your eyes or threatening to levy a punishment? Or did other, internal impulses play a role, such as wanting your kids to be happy, the satisfaction or pride you take in them, wanting to meet a deadline at work, or a desire to feel connected with others through your work? What *really* got you to comply? If you think it through, chances are you didn't take action because some external force compelled you to do so. Rather, you did it because on some level you felt internal motivation, and because you had the thinking skills at your disposal—relating to self-control, for instance, or perspective taking, or the ability to think through the likely consequences of your actions—that allowed you to perform the unpleasant action.

order to sit still, tune out distractions, think through the consequences of not doing it, and actually get work done. Lack of compliance is rarely just a matter of wanting to or not, any more than compliance is (see the above exercise, Rethinking "Good" Behavior).

The same reasoning applies to the world of adult behavior.

Why do some employees spend hours at their boring jobs checking social media when they know they're not supposed to? "Because they want to," we say, as a prelude to reprimanding them. But few employees (if any) would rather work at a boring job than connect with their friends on social media. Some can and do forgo Facebook, and it's because they're *able* to, while their less compliant colleagues aren't. To understand this latter group, we need to question what skills or aptitudes those who exhibit challenging behaviors might lack.

When we think about the many other explanations people give for challenging behavior, we find that they are specious. "Oh," we might say, "he just wants attention." Who *doesn't* want attention? And why would someone behave poorly to get attention if he possesses the skills to do so in a more positive way? It doesn't make sense—unless of course these individuals *couldn't* just as easily behave well. Relatedly, people will look at someone's bad behavior and say, "Negative attention is better than no attention." That's ridiculous. Everyone I've ever met would prefer to have no attention than to anger or alienate others, bringing punishment upon themselves.

People will also say, "Mike just wants his own way. He wants control." Join the club! Show me the person who prefers other people's ways, I think to myself as I ask what they mean. They respond, "He works really hard to try to get what he needs." We *all* try to get our needs met, some more adeptly and graciously than others. Or they'll say, "Mike is a manipulator. He's an *expert* manipulator." When people accuse someone of being an expert manipulator, I tell them that if this person really were such an expert manipulator, he'd be so good that you wouldn't *know* you were being manipulated. Instead, that person is behaving poorly because he lacks the ability to get what he wants without frustrating those around him. We all want our own way! Some of us just have a harder time handling it when we don't get it.

COMMON DEAD-END EXPLANATIONS FOR CHALLENGING BEHAVIOR

The following dead-end explanations are either inaccurate or unhelpful (in that they don't point us to actions we can take to address the behavior). Do any look familiar? Have you thought or said these things about someone in your life?

"He just wants attention."

"She just wants her own way."

"He just wants control."

"He's manipulative."

"He has a bad attitude."

"She's making bad choices."

"He won't cooperate."

"She has a mental illness."*

"She was adopted."*

"He is the child of an alcoholic."*

"She had an abusive husband."*

* Possibly accurate statement that doesn't help us.

Finally, people will look down on someone who behaves in challenging ways by saying, "She's making bad choices." That implies that this offender is weighing her options, projecting them into the future, and saying: "Okay, this course of action would be a good choice. That course of action would be a bad choice. What should I do? I'm going to make a bad choice." This almost never transpires in the mind of the person making the bad choices. Instead, she is more likely having a hard time with the type of thinking required to weigh choices, generate alternatives, and think ahead about possible outcomes. She might also lack the skills necessary to perform the actual behavior that the "right choice" would entail. Thinking *skill, not will* shifts our focus from dead-end explanations to things we can actually change.

Paradigm Shift

You might review my argument thus far and counter, "*Skill, not will* sounds good for routine bad behavior, but certainly when people commit serious crimes, those people intend to do harm." Actually, even most serious crimes are best understood not as a matter of will but in terms of skill. If you spend any time talking to criminal offenders, you realize that the vast majority commit crimes because they're trying to address important concerns but can't figure out a better way to do so. It is easy to say that people shouldn't steal when you have money to buy food. Spend a day in the shoes of someone who doesn't know where his next meal is coming from and you may think differently. These individuals often require impressive cognitive skills to handle the issues, difficulties, or dilemmas they face, and if they lack those skills, they break the law and frequently cause harm. Few people *want* to break the law. More than a few can't find a better way.

Years ago, I interviewed a young adult in a correctional facility who had shot someone and was on trial for attempted murder. I made the mistake of asking what he was thinking when he pulled the trigger. The young man leaned in toward me so that our faces were just inches apart. "Dude," he said, "that's the stupidest fucking question anybody's ever asked me."

"Um, okay," I said. "Do you mind telling me why that's the stupidest question anybody has asked you?"

He leaned in even closer. My heart was racing. "Do you think if I was thinking I would have fucking done it?"

That one moment taught me as much as two years of graduate school classes. *Of course* he wasn't thinking. If he had been thinking, he wouldn't have pulled the trigger. This young man, like virtually all people who perpetrate criminal acts, knew the difference between right and wrong, and he knew the consequences of shooting someone. But the smart part of his brain (what is referred to as the prefrontal cortex) was closed for business in that moment and he was operating from a place much lower down in the brain, the same place that provides our fight-or-flight instincts. No amount of jail time would have deterred this man from behaving violently. For that, he would need to improve his impulse control and frustration tolerance skills, or as professionals call them, emotion and self-regulation skills.

It often seems that people are misbehaving on purpose, but that's because we're trained to interpret offending acts that way. It's also because *we're* upset. Whether we're a parent, a teacher, a manager, a prison guard, or any other authority figure, challenging behavior can be immensely frustrating to experience. In many cases, the offender is causing us pain. Caught up in the moment, we can't expect ourselves to piece together the complex reasons for his or her behavior. We feel disrespected, aggravated, and overwhelmed. Our authority has been challenged. We feel like lashing out and teaching the offender "a lesson"—and we often do. We hit back and place blame. When entire communities become upset, we see a similar kind of response, with calls for police and judges to lay down the law and get tough on crime. The irony, of course, is that we *do* want to teach people—not a lesson, but thinking skills.

We are entitled to feel frustration, fear, and anger. They're entirely understandable emotions. But our emotions hamper our rationality and judgment. As you probably know from your own life, people who are upset are not in the best position to assess a situation objectively and generate practical solutions. Think of the last time you got upset. Maybe it was at that seemingly obnoxious driver who cut you off. Or at your colleague who said something unflattering about you to your boss. Were you thinking calmly in the moment? Did you come up with a practical solution that would pass the "tomorrow" test (i.e., when you wake up tomorrow and are calm once again, will the solution still seem like a good idea)? Or did you lash out? Be honest!

Lashing out at offenders by blaming them, saying they did it on purpose, and punishing them harshly may provide relief in the moment, but it never solves the problem. It's far more constructive to assume that someone is struggling with an under-lying skill and proceed from there. The vast majority of the time, a skills deficit *is* the issue. And if you're wrong, you won't have lost much. On the other hand, if you wrongly assume the worst about someone's intentions, you *will* have lost much. As we'll see later, the downsides of traditional punishment are significant, including the inescapable fact that they simply don't work.

Skeptics might contend that some people *do* commit shoot-ings and other crimes willfully, putting a great deal of rational thought into them. The horrific, premeditated mass killings that have riled so many U.S. communities would appear to have been committed in this way, as would terrorist attacks perpetrated by followers of ISIS and other groups. In truth, despite these un-speakably tragic atrocities, it is worth noting that pure proactive aggression is rare—much rarer than people think.[5] The vast ma-jority of the time, criminal acts arise out of poor responses to frustration on the part of criminals (what is called reactive ag-gression) or other failures in people's basic cognitive skills. Even proactive aggression from someone with good impulse control can be the result of struggles with skills like perspective taking and empathizing. Nevertheless, our criminal justice system, like most of our institutions, contents itself with addressing moti-vation alone.

Years ago, when my colleague Ross Greene, PhD,[6] and I began working in a correctional system in rural Maine, we pre-sented our *skill, not will* approach to one of the frontline man-agers. This man was a big, grizzled character and a huge skeptic. Seeing us as a couple of ivory-tower, elbow-patch types from Harvard, he made it clear that he believed the proper way of handling juvenile offenders was tough love. "What you're saying about skills could be useful for a couple of the kids here," he said, "like maybe two or three out of a hundred. But most of the kids here are sociopaths. They're simply not going to respond, and they will take advantage of you if you let them. You can't change them."

Despite his misgivings, this manager was willing to try something new, so he and his colleagues worked with us to implement our seemingly softer, skills-oriented approach to discipline. Five years later, recidivism at their facility had plummeted, and this skeptic had become a true believer. When people asked him whether focusing on skills really worked, he would say, "Every once in a while, I come across a real sociopath, but we're talking two or three kids out of a hundred." It was a complete turnaround. This leader became much more alert to the complexity of bad behavior, much more compassionate toward and understanding of offenders, and, best of all, much more effective at his job. He realized that virtually *all* challenging behavior arises from a problem with skills, not motivation. And that realization means that virtually all behavior is changeable if you can help people build the skills they lack.

As this example suggests, *skill, not will* is not just a different approach to discipline. It's a change in mind-set, a paradigm shift that could apply to anyone's behavior in any context—your child's, your colleague's, your neighbor's, your spouse's. Rather than blaming offenders and "bringing down the hammer," we challenge ourselves to reflect on the offender's concerns and address the underlying causes of bad behavior. We also push ourselves to set aside our own emotions and become calmer and more rational in handling behavior we dislike. The logic, again, is simple: If someone *could* change, they *would* change. The question is not whether someone is willing to change. It is whether he is *able* to change. What's standing in his way, if he's not doing well, is not a lack of effort or motivation but a lack of skill that needs to be understood and addressed. Nobody who misbehaves *prefers* doing poorly to doing well. So rather than resort to rewards and punishments, let's figure out which specific skill struggles are playing a role, and take steps to remedy them—to help bring about meaningful, lasting change.

> If someone *could* change, they *would* change.

Seeing Challenging Behavior as a Learning Disability

My grandfather, in his 102nd year as of this writing, has many colorful aphorisms from his childhood in Tupelo, Mississippi. One of my favorites is his astute remark that "if you give a dog a name, eventually he'll answer to it." If you tell misbehaving people that they're bad—lazy, unmotivated, purposely difficult, deserving of punishment—they'll start to believe that, and they'll start to look, talk, and act like lazy, unmotivated people who are purposely difficult and deserving of punishment. They'll lose any drive to change or improve. However, if you tell a misbehaving person that everyone is working on something, and that we all struggle with certain thinking skills we need to handle daily life, she won't feel demonized or demoralized. She'll see a path open up in front of her and feel optimistic that she is able to change her life for the better.

For decades, we used to cast judgment on people who struggled in school with subjects like reading and math. We used to tell them that they were lazy and unmotivated, and we used to punish or reward them in an effort to fire up their motivation. Likewise, when we encountered people who were hyper, impulsive, and unfocused, we dismissed them as misfits and applied conventional discipline. In both cases, we lost generations of young people who grew up feeling beaten down, convinced that they were lazy, stupid, difficult, and just plain *bad*.

As we now know, many of these people were suffering from dyslexia, ADHD, and other learning disabilities that originate in brain functioning. These kids were trying harder than their peers to learn or function—they wanted desperately to succeed. Yet we punished them because we perceived motivation as the issue. Because we applied traditional discipline, we took a problem— deficits in thinking skills—and made it much worse. I'm certain some readers of this book know firsthand how difficult it is to be the student in class trying harder than anyone else to succeed, and yet still being treated as not trying hard enough.

Instead of casting judgment on challenging behavior, let's start treating it for what it truly is: a learning disability every bit as real as dyslexia. Whereas others might struggle with reading or with paying attention, people who behave in challenging ways struggle with skills like flexibility, frustration tolerance, and problem solving. Like individuals with dyslexia or ADHD, people who exhibit challenging behavior are often trying *harder* than others to get along and behave well, and they're failing because they just don't have the skills. I know because I've seen hundreds of people just like this in my practice. I've also collaborated with numerous professionals in schools, prisons, police departments, and treatment programs who work with challenging kids and adults, and we are always able to trace the challenging behavior back to underlying skills deficits. Finally, I've seen the science, which plainly shows that skills deficits and underlying differences in brain development give rise to challenging behavior.

In addition to regarding challenging behavior as a learning disability, we could also frame it as a developmental delay. Have you ever parented or even just spent time around a two- or three-year-old? Then you know that no child at that age behaves well. During the terrible twos, kids bite. They kick. They hit. They scream. They run. They throw themselves on the floor and howl. All this drama occurs because toddlers don't have anything else in their repertoire. They are terrible at all of the skills I've been talking about: solving problems, tolerating frustration, and being flexible. Toddlers are the *last* people with whom you'd want to try negotiating a conflict. At the least instigation, they go ballistic. As for flexibility, forget it. Depart from their usual routine, and the drama starts up.

Most six-year-old children behave better than toddlers, most fourteen-year-olds behave better than six-year-olds, and most eighteen-year-olds behave better than fourteen-year-olds. That's because as most children grow, their skills in the areas of problem solving, frustration tolerance, and flexibility grow as well, in lockstep with their brain development. But in *some* people, skills in one or more of these areas don't develop in line with the norms. These kids might be fifteen yet have the frustration tolerance of a five-year-old. They might be twenty-two and have the problem-solving skills of an eight-year-old. Or they might be full-grown adults in their fifties and have the flexibility of a ten-year-old. People of any age can struggle with delays or weaknesses in cognitive skills, and it is never too late to build one's skills.

Reframing challenging behavior as either a disability or a delay doesn't just help people feel better about themselves. It transforms how authority figures think about their roles and responses when confronted with misbehavior. Rather than try to change the offender's motivations, we can start to help people who behave in challenging ways comprehend why they are struggling and then build up their skills so they can do better in the future. We can assess which specific skills they lack and then work on an individualized basis to teach those skills. *Skill, not will* allows for *us* to become more empathic. Instead of the stern *might makes right* model of authority, we can embrace a new model that puts us in the role of supportive collaborators, teachers, and coaches.

I've argued that many of the common explanations for challenging behavior defy logic. But when we interpret challenging behavior as a learning disability, we realize that still other common explanations might have some truth to them, yet comparatively lack practical relevance. For example, bosses, parents, teachers, judges, and other authority figures might explain away bad behavior by noting that the offender was adopted, or suffered trauma, or that he had a mother who drank while pregnant. Those explanations, while possibly accurate, don't tell us how to help. They don't move us closer to a solution.

Let's put those explanations to what I call the explanation litmus test. Pick any time frame and use this prompt: "In such-and-such number of months, we hope that s/he will be better at . . ." Fill in the blank with your explanation and see how it sounds. "In six months, I hope she's better at her fetal alcohol syndrome." That doesn't sound terribly helpful. Likewise, someone might well have been adopted and could have struggled with attachment issues as a result, but knowing this offers no path forward to achieving progress now. Nothing we do now can change the situation. It's not clinically useful information.

Seeing challenging behavior as a learning disability or a delay *does* pass the explanation litmus test. If we analyze a person and discover that, for instance, he struggles to stay calm when frustrated, we can start building up that skill, much as we build up our muscles at the gym. With practice and hard work, the offender will see improvement in six months. With continued practice, he'll see even more progress after another six months. Interpreting the offender's behavior as the result of a learning disability is no more or less truthful than interpreting it as a lingering result of childhood trauma or fetal alcohol syndrome, but it is far more helpful. It points us toward clear actions we can take to make a difference and reminds us that all offenders are changeable.

In the end, regarding challenging behavior as a disability or delay—as *skill, not will*—is a far more humane approach. It forces you to realize the truth: that people who behave poorly often are trying harder than most. They're hurting already, and the last thing they need is to suffer the additional pain and humiliation of conventional punishment—particularly punishment that doesn't work.

If you still find yourself believing that people can change if they simply *want* it badly enough, then I have something I'd like to tell you about. Eight-year-old Jennifer was the oldest sibling in a fairly affluent family living in a Boston suburb. She began experiencing problems with reading, as well as problems with organizing and planning—what we call executive function disabilities. As she worked her way through the third, fourth, and fifth grades, her schoolwork became harder and she struggled to organize her homework. Upset about that, she began acting out—fighting with her siblings, behaving disrespectfully to her teachers at school, and so on.

Jennifer's teachers perceived that she was trying to get her way and draw attention to herself, so they responded the only way they knew how. They cracked down, putting her on a behavior intervention plan at school that applied punishments when she misbehaved and offered rewards when she behaved well. Jennifer's behavior worsened, and now we know why: Her underlying skills didn't improve, and on top of that, she was dealing with the burden of interventions that were supposed to help but only made her feel even worse about herself.

Jennifer's parents brought her to see me in my office. She wasn't eager to talk, but she would write. Here is what she scrawled in red Magic Marker: "My brain is iteotic [*sic*]. I make stupid mistakes. I mess everthing [*sic*] up. I always make a mess and get hurt and ruin everything." This wasn't a kid who was doing it on purpose, who was an expert manipulator, who just wanted to get her own way. This was a kid in pain, a kid who wanted to do well but couldn't. Jennifer's self-confidence had eroded because of her inability to adapt to the expectations of those around her, and because of the negative messages her parents and teachers were unwittingly sending by treating her behavior as willful. The danger, as so often happens, was that Jennifer would eventually give up and stop trying to change her behavior. She'd say to herself, "Geez, maybe all these adults are right. Maybe I really am not trying hard. Maybe I really am lazy. After all, why else would they be trying to motivate me?" If you give a dog a name, eventually she will answer to it. This girl was already answering to it at the age of eight.

Every time I look at the note Jennifer wrote to me, I feel galvanized all over again to spread the message of *skill, not will*. These poor kids think they're "idiotic" and that they "ruin everything." They believe it's "all their fault." Can you imagine how awful that must feel? It can take a lifetime to overcome self-perceptions like that, if one ever really does. People like Jennifer aren't bad. Like all of us, they've got skills that need work. Unfortunately for them, their skills deficits produce behavior that pushes our buttons and leads to misunderstanding.

From Problem Child to Class President

When we shift our mind-sets and approach challenging behavior as a skills deficit, amazing things happen. Remember Susan from the beginning of this chapter? In Susan's case, her parents stopped trying to force her to go to school using conventional discipline. Recognizing the role played by her cognitive inflexibility, we instead found ways to help her develop flexible thinking skills. I worked with the vice principal, the guidance counselor, and the school psychologist to understand what made her tick, enumerating the specific flexibility skills she lacked and describing how certain situations conspired with her inflexibility to create a blowup. The solution was twofold. First, we needed to create contingency plans for when Susan developed migraines. That way she could go to school secure in the knowledge that she would know exactly what to do if a migraine struck. If she had a template, she wouldn't freak out. Second, we needed to figure out ways to help build her flexibility skills over time, so that we could reduce the risk of future behavioral problems as new situations in her life emerged.

We implemented both parts of this solution. We created an intricate contingency plan together with Susan, specifying that she would consult the school secretary if she had a migraine. To spare Susan embarrassment in front of her friends, the secretary wouldn't ask Susan any questions. When Susan got migraines, she was in too much pain to speak clearly, and she wound up feeling self-conscious about what she said. The secretary would take Susan to the guidance counselor, who would let Susan use the phone to call her mother, again without asking questions. We went on to specify whom Susan would call if her mom didn't pick up, and how long she would wait to see whether the migraine went away before the school sent her home for the day. It was all there on paper with Susan as coauthor, and it helped Susan feel much more comfortable about going to school.

As for the second part of the solution, we didn't have to embark on a whole new process. As we'll see, the best way to build skills that are absent or lacking when people misbehave is to give people real-life practice in solving problems. As problems arise, parents, teachers, counselors, and other authority figures can collaborate with individuals to craft solutions rather than simply imposing their will. The process of working things out builds new skills, and actually forms new connections in the brain. In Susan's case, the beginning of skill building was to involve her in creating the contingency plan the school put in place for her. As we created the plan, parents, teachers, and administrators didn't dictate the terms, and neither did Susan, who had to practice her flexibility skills. There was a process of give-and-take, during which Susan got just a little bit better in her ability to deviate from her ingrained perceptions of how things should be. That's how skills are built: little by little, with authority figures serving as coaches and helpers.

We reintegrated Susan back into her school over a matter of weeks. Over several months, we got her to a point where she could fully engage with school and do well. She finished her first year in middle school without major behavioral issues. Six months later, when she was in her second year, Susan's family moved to California. If any event would upset a kid with flexibility issues, it would be a move clear across the country. But thanks to the ongoing work Susan and her family had done to build her skills and give her coping strategies, she handled it well. A year or so later, Susan's parents got in touch with me to let me know that she was elected president of her class.

Perceiving Susan's challenging behavior in terms of *skill, not will* enabled us to find both a short-term fix and a long-term solution. All of us learned to be more empathic, collaborative, and flexible (and, in fact, research shows that teachers often become more empathic when learning about a student's cognitive skills deficits as opposed to just his or her challenging behavior).[7] We learned to build the underlying cognitive skills rather than slap on another punishment or bestow another reward. And we learned to return to the original meaning of the word *discipline*. In America, we so often use that word as synonymous with *punishment*, and yet the original definition of *discipline* is very different. It means "to teach." Let's all shift the way we think about discipline. Let's return to the original definition of the word, whether we are talking about school, the workplace, or at home with our kids or partner. In the next chapter, I'll review the large body of science that says we should.

CHAPTER TWO

The Science Behind Challenging Behavior

Here's a challenge to try with your friends at your next dinner party. Write down five random numbers between 0 and 9. Read the numbers slowly to your friends—for example, "8," "6," "9," "4," "2." Challenge your friends to repeat the numbers back to you in the order you just read them. Can they do it? Chances are they can, and after a couple of drinks no less. But here's where it gets good: Try the exercise again, reading a new set of five numbers to them, just like you did before. This time, see if they can recite the numbers *backward*. Can they do it? Some of them probably can. But can they do it with a set of seven random numbers? Or ten?

I perform this exercise with audiences during trainings, and it's hysterical. I see people grimacing, their eyes shut, trying to perform this simple, little task. They point up in the air with their fingers and draw little numbers in an attempt to remember and keep everything in order.

Psychologists call this exercise the digit span test, and they use it to gauge people's attention and working memory skills.[1] Psychologists used to think most adults could absorb and hold roughly five things in their heads at once. Later they revised that, asserting that an average adult could absorb and hold seven items (words, numbers, tasks, etc.).[2] Phone numbers today are ten digits long, which most people would find extremely hard to remember. Yet most of us can recall telephone numbers using a mental trick. If we familiarize ourselves with the area code, we have to remember only eight items—the seven numbers of the primary phone number plus the area code.

The digit span test might seem like a cute little parlor game, but it's more than that. We don't use attention and working memory just to recall phone numbers. We also use it to help us get along in our daily lives. When we aren't good at paying attention and remembering, we run afoul of parents, bosses, and other authority figures. If you're a kid with a very limited working memory as measured by the digit span test (i.e., you might be able to remember only three numbers at a time), you're going to strain to hold a directive in your head such as "Go upstairs and get your backpack. Come back downstairs. Lock the door, don't forget your jacket, and meet me outside." If you're an adult, you'll have a hard time holding on to "I need that report by the end of the day. Make sure it's on card stock, because it's got to be on the thick stuff. I don't want it double sided, okay? And I want it single spaced. Oh, and I need it e-mailed to me by four as well."

The digit span test is only one of a number of tests that allow psychologists to assess what we call neurocognitive skills. These are an array of thinking skills related to the general areas of flexibility, frustration tolerance, and problem solving. Since the 1960s, researchers have used tests like the Stroop Color and Word Test (which measures how well a person can control their impulses) and the Boston Naming Test (which measures a person's language fluency) to study neurocognitive skills in populations of children and adults.[3]

Researchers have found that some people are far above average in these skills, while others fall significantly below average. And they've found something else: People who exhibit chronically challenging behavior tend to struggle developmentally in one or more of these areas, and the most challenging people struggle across many (or all) areas of neurocognitive skill. In other words, scientists have long established what the vast majority of us overlook in our everyday lives: that *skill, not will* underlies most instances of bad behavior.

During the late 1980s, researchers in London gathered together a group of four-year-olds whose parents had rated them as hard to manage, and they also assembled another group of preschoolers without behavioral difficulties as a control. They administered neurocognitive tests to measure the children's key executive functioning skills: the ability to control their impulses, the ability to shift between tasks, and the ability to retain information (working memory). The hard-to-manage kids were much worse at controlling their impulses, although they were about as good as the control group at shifting between tasks and working memory.[4]

In another study, researchers tested 182 children in the first and second grades to measure how skilled they were in processing their emotions. In particular, they tested how well the children could perceive emotional states, whether they tended to register some emotions more than others, and how good they were at experiencing others' emotions (empathy). Analyzing the data, researchers found that kids who weren't as fluent in multiple emotional processing skills were more likely to behave aggressively (as reported by their teachers).[5] These are just two of countless studies that all show similar findings: Subjects who exhibit challenging behavior fare much worse on neurocognitive tasks.[6]

Probing the Sources of Bad Behavior

If studies such as these are so numerous and the results are so consistent in favor of *skill, not will*, why does conventional discipline remain pervasive? It's incredible when you think about it: In this area of life, our practice diverges almost entirely from what science tells us—it's as if the science doesn't exist. Imagine if almost everyone, even people who claimed to be health conscious, continued to smoke even after decades of research from multiple angles had determined smoking to be harmful.

In part, I think we continue to treat behavior as a matter of will because authority figures don't know how else to think about it. If you're a parent, a teacher, or a manager, the main tools you have for addressing bad behavior are the usual, age-old rewards and punishments. If those were no longer available, how would you handle a person who isn't doing what you expect them to do? As mentioned in the last chapter, bad behavior also arouses an emotional response in authority figures. It's so hurtful or offensive to us that we want to lash out and punish it, and we have trouble imagining another way.

We also continue to think of misbehavior as will, not skill, because many people don't *know* about the science. Although neurocognitive research has existed for decades, it's fairly fragmented in the scientific literature, not something a popular audience can easily access and understand. Researchers in the field are often not familiar with one another's work. Some researchers might have tested for thinking skills while studying attention deficit hyperactivity disorder (ADHD), for instance, others while studying social skills, still others while studying skills related to the regulation of emotions. These are all separate bodies of literature, existing in what amount to intellectual silos. So while the evidence for *skill, not will* has been accumulating, few people have stepped back, noticed the bigger picture, and publicized its implications.

I first became aware of the bigger picture of *skill, not will* during the early 1990s, while I was preparing to apply to graduate school. To gain more real-life experience and buttress my application, I took a job at Massachusetts General Hospital as a research assistant working in the lab of Dr. Joseph Biederman, one of the world's leading ADHD experts. At the time, the psychiatric profession was just beginning to regard ADHD as a legitimate diagnosis, in large part due to Dr. Biederman's research. Medical science knew little about the condition, and many people still regarded people with ADHD as willfully misbehaving rather than suffering from an underlying neurological condition. Dr. Biederman and his lab were trying to determine if children with ADHD also suffered from other psychiatric disorders, like depression, anxiety, oppositional defiant disorder (a recurrent pattern of hostile or defiant behavior), developmental disorders such as those on the autism spectrum, speech and language issues, and so on. If ADHD *did* coincide with other disorders, it should affect how caregivers should treat the condition.

In performing the research, we compiled a sample of families with a child diagnosed with clear ADHD and a random sample of families from the community that didn't have a child diagnosed with ADHD and matched for factors like socioeconomic differences, age, and gender.[7] My job, and that of my fellow research assistants, was to hop in a rented Honda Accord and drive around Massachusetts interviewing families. We wanted to see if the kids in each sample suffered from other disorders and compare results across the two groups. When we arrived at a given house, we didn't know if we were going to interview a family whose child had ADHD or one whose child didn't suffer from that disorder because study staff were "blinded" so as to not let any of our biases influence the results. Yet we played a game among ourselves of trying to guess, basing our judgments on the messiness of the house (suggesting possible organizational or planning issues) or whether the parent seemed to struggle with maintaining attention (the disorder has a strong genetic component).

Every week we came in from the field, sat down with child psychiatrists on Dr. Biederman's team, and reported the interview results to the doctors. We evaluated which emotional and behavioral symptoms each child had, if any. I was not surprised to learn that kids diagnosed with ADHD had a much greater chance of *also* having severe behavioral problems compared with kids in the control group. Conversely—and here's the critical point—kids diagnosed with oppositional defiant disorder also experienced much higher rates of other kinds of disorders, such as speech or language deficits, mood disorders, and so on. In fact, it was extremely rare to find a kid who was chronically misbehaving but *not* suffering from other problems. In professional jargon, we call this psychiatric comorbidity, the coexistence of disorders.

Although I was just out of college and didn't yet know about the neuroscience research being done, I found myself wondering how to interpret the clustering of these different conditions. Maybe the diverse behavior and psychological problems these kids faced *derived from a variety of skills deficits they were experiencing.* Take a child with behavior issues who also was experiencing language delays (our research turned up many kids like this). Speech and language skills are *integral* to our ability to tolerate frustration in the world and to solve problems. If you're an eight-year-old kid who can't communicate what's bothering you or understand what others are communicating, you might only be as skilled as a three-year-old in your ability to enlist others to help solve the problem. Conflict situations become that much more frustrating and difficult. Whereas other eight-year-olds might behave adaptively when things don't go their way, you react by blowing up. An adult might perceive this as a behavior issue, when really the behavioral difficulties are just the downstream effect of being weak in language and communication skills.

Tracking the Skills

Less than a decade later, I was out of graduate school and fortunate to be working with a colleague, Dr. Ross Greene, who was developing a new approach to treating children with behavioral problems. Greene sought a concise way of summarizing and operationalizing the research findings in our field. The past several decades of science—hundreds of studies performed all over the world with all kinds of people as subjects—showed that people with challenging behavior lacked skills in at least one of five primary skills categories: language and communication skills, attention and working memory skills, emotion and self-regulation skills, cognitive flexibility skills, and social thinking skills.[8] Greene published a book called *The Explosive Child*, and in the years that followed, he and I explored the ways these skills contribute to challenging behavior in our clinical work with families and institutions.

What have we learned since then? Let's take a look at these skill categories one at a time.

Language and Communication Skills: The Meaning of "I Don't Give a Shit"

Language and communication skills are essential to handling life's challenges and behaving well.[9] It's hardly surprising that the majority of children with specific language disorders also have psychiatric issues and behavioral difficulties.[10] As an illustration, think of kids in the midst of their "terrible twos." How skilled are misbehaving two-year-olds at communication? Not very. As a result, they can't engage in negotiations (even pretty simple ones) to resolve disputes. Thankfully, most four-, six-, and eight-year-olds have better language and communication skills that enable them to solve problems. This may be the primary reason we don't have something called the "terrible eights"!

Both children and adults with language and communication issues can become easily frustrated when unable to express their concerns. Sometimes this frustration leads to explosive behavior, but it can also lead to what adults might regard as passive-aggressive behavior. The person stares at you without speaking, seemingly obstinate and refusing to respond. In fact, she may *want* to respond but she either can't find the words or is slow to process them. As I've seen in my practice, older kids (and some adults) will sometimes compensate for language and communication deficits by saying things like "This is stupid." They don't think it's stupid, but they're used to the world not giving them enough time to process speech. They've learned that it's easier just to dismiss someone or something as stupid.

I once had a teenage patient who would respond "I don't give a shit" whenever I tried to engage him in conversation. "Hey, I heard something happened in school yesterday," I'd say. "Can you fill me in?"

He'd scowl at me and say, "I don't give a shit."

"Well, you might not care, but we sort of need to figure this out. I want to make sure I understand your perspective, so just tell me: What was happening?"

"I don't give a shit. Fuck you."

This was a typical conversation for this kid—one of the reasons his parents had brought him to see me. For months, I couldn't figure out what was going on. His constant negativity frustrated me, but I tried to practice what I preached and focused on identifying his skill struggles. Eventually, I wondered if he was having language and communication issues, even though he had never been formally diagnosed with a speech or language disability. One day in my office I said to him, "Hey, when I ask you about something that has happened to you, what's going on in your brain? Like, literally, what are you thinking about?"

He sat for a while in silence, pondering. "Well, I start to think about what you asked."

"Okay," I said. "So why don't you ever say that?"

He shrugged. "I don't know."

"Well, you say you don't care."

(Pause.) "Yeah, I don't really mean that."

"If you don't mean it, why do you say it?"

(Pause.) "To make the conversation stop."

I continued this line of questioning, and we discovered that the reason he didn't like to talk with parents, teachers, or others was because nobody gave him enough time to process the information. They weren't rushing him out of impatience or a lack of empathy. They were assuming that he was *refusing* to respond. Later, when I asked him to fill me in on what happened the day before, and I waited patiently for him to speak, we sat in silence for forty-five seconds before he answered. In the context of a conversation, that's an eternity. (Try it yourself: Remain silent for forty-five seconds after someone asks you a question.) But at the end of those forty-five seconds, he offered a clear, well-formulated thought. "I don't give a shit" had been a compensatory strategy, or as people in a business context might say, a work-around. What he was *really* trying to say was: "There's no way in hell this adult is going to give me enough time to process what he just asked me and then to formulate a response using language. So let's just call the whole thing off."

Other patients with slow language-processing skills whom I've treated might have seemed like they were flat-out ignoring what their parents and other authority figures were asking or talking to them about. A mother might ask her son, "Charlie, come to dinner!" Hearing this, Charlie thinks to himself: *Okay, she wants me to come to dinner.* Then he thinks: *Ah, so that means you want me to turn off the TV.* Then he thinks: *But I'm twenty minutes into this show. I would sort of like to see how it turns out.*

By the time he's thought these things, ten seconds have passed. His mother has been watching to see if he will comply with her request, and when she sees no action, she understandably assumes he's refusing to respond, being difficult, or not listening. She's upset, so she storms into the family room to grab the remote. But Charlie meant no harm. He just couldn't process words and thus his own internal thoughts as quickly as people around him expected him to.

LANGUAGE AND COMMUNICATION SKILLS

➤ Understands spoken directions
➤ Understands and follows conversations
➤ Expresses concerns, needs, or thoughts in words
➤ Is able to tell someone what's bothering him/her

Attention and Working Memory Skills: Secrets of a Messy Office

A second category, attention and working memory skills, covers a range of different skills, including attention, working memory, the ability to tune out distractions, and the ability to plan and organize. *Driven to Distraction*, a book by Drs. Edward M. Hallowell and John J. Ratey, was among the first to describe to a lay audience the importance of being able to maintain your focus when required to do so, and the difficulty that some people have with that skill.[11] Focus and related skills, often referred to as executive functions, tend to be highly correlated, so if someone is found to be struggling with one of them—say, working memory—chances are their organization skills are weak as well. Each is intertwined with the other. My old mentor, Dr. Joseph Biederman, called this the "cockroach principle"—where there is one, there are many. Not the best visual, but it's an apt metaphor.

In any case, let's return to working memory. We've seen how working memory helps us remember phone numbers, but consider what happens every time you carry on a simple conversation. You might encounter a friend at the grocery store and stop to say hello. While your friend speaks, you're saying to yourself, *Let me listen to what this person is saying.* You might not be interested in what she's saying, but you pay attention anyway (a skill). As she speaks, you're also thinking, *Okay, what do I think about what this person is saying?* And you're thinking, *What could I or should I say based on what I think about what I think this person is saying?* And you also might think, *How do I think this person will respond to what I might say or do based on what I am thinking about what she is saying?*

That's a *lot* of stuff to keep in mind at once. As we go about our daily lives, our minds are working way more than we could ever fathom. So if your executive functioning skills, like working memory and attention, are weak, you might well have trouble partaking in even the most casual of conversations.[12]

Another set of skills that plays a critically important role in behavior is planning and organization, which rely heavily on decent working memory skills. Sometimes couples fight over messiness in the house. Typically, the neat and organized person complains about the messy tendencies of their partner. When I delve into this, I typically find that their partner lacks organization or planning skills. It's not "just" that they leave things around. It's often that they struggle with the skills required to clean up or stay organized. If you tell a person with strong organizational skills to clean their office, they'll approach the task logically, starting with the big tasks and working from there. They'll first pick up the stacks of paper from the floor, understanding that once they've done that, they'll be able to clean the rest of the office much more easily. If you ask a person who struggles with organizational and planning skills to clean their office, they might step over the stacks of paper, hop on the chair, reach up to a shelf, and start dusting the pictures in the top right corner. In other words, they struggle to know *how* to plan, organize, and execute a relatively simple task like cleaning a room.

These everyday behavioral differences show up as *brain* differences when we do neuropsychological testing. The Rey-Osterrieth Complex Figure task asks people to study a complex figure comprised of different geometric shapes. People with solid organizational and planning skills see the outline of the figure and memorize that first. They then fill in the details around it. Others who struggle with these skills see small details but have trouble seeing the bigger picture. When asked to recall the figure from memory, they can't describe an overarching, organizational structure. All they can point to is random, disconnected details. Just imagine what a person like this would do if you gave him a complex academic problem or business task to tackle. He would inevitably become disoriented and frustrated. Chances are his performance would suffer.

ATTENTION AND WORKING MEMORY SKILLS

➤ Stays with tasks requiring sustained attention
➤ Does things in a logical sequence or set order
➤ Keeps track of time; correctly assesses how much time a task will take
➤ Reflects on multiple thoughts or ideas at the same time
➤ Maintains focus during activities
➤ Ignores irrelevant noises, people, or other stimuli; tunes things out when necessary
➤ Considers multiple options for solutions to a problem

Emotion and Self-regulation Skills: Why Gym Class Doesn't Work

The third category, emotion and self-regulation skills, covers abilities related to people's management or control of themselves and their feelings.[13] How well does a person deal with frustration or other intense emotions? Do their emotions go from zero to sixty in the snap of a finger? Research has shown that people with poor emotion regulation become "cognitively debilitated"— they can't think clearly. Falling prey to a storm of uncontrollable emotions, they fall into severe temper tantrums or episodes of rage.[14] Not surprisingly, they also have a hard time solving problems. Doing so, after all, requires that once you experience an unpleasant emotion (which informs you that there is a problem that requires solving), you quickly dampen that emotion in order to activate your cerebral cortex (the smart part of the brain responsible for rational thought) so you can think clearly. This second step proves difficult for people who struggle with emotion regulation skills. As psychologists say, they become dysregulated— a fancy word for "upset quickly."

Included within the general category of self-regulation is a very important skill: impulse control, or the ability to stop and think before acting. To appreciate how important impulse control is, close your eyes and consider what happened yesterday. Imagine that as you went through the day, you thought or did the *very first thing* that came to mind. It's pretty funny to imagine this, but pretty frightening, too. Even the most minor interaction between two people requires constant impulse control. If none of us had that control, our world would be a very different place, because our first impulse in any situation is thankfully often not the one we follow. Some people unfortunately go with their first impulse because they have an unusually hard time controlling themselves. One of my teenage patients once told me, "I really have no idea what I'm thinking until I say it out loud." That's terrible. This teen can't prevent himself from doing or saying the first thing his impulses tell him. I don't know about you, but I really don't want most people knowing the first thing that goes through my mind at any given moment!

One of the saddest ironies about people with poor impulse control is that they tend to get hit with more punishments than anyone else. Why is that ironic? Because consequences require decent impulse control to work in the first place! A negative consequence can remediate a person's behavior only if she *has* the impulse control to make use of the consequence. The next time around, she has to be able to stop midstream, remember the negative consequence she experienced last time, and resolve to behave differently this time. People with impulse control issues frequently become trapped in spirals of bad behavior and punishment that are difficult to break and that lead to nowhere good.

> Consequences require decent impulse control to work in the first place!

Some people struggle with another self-regulation skill: the ability to adjust their levels of emotional or physiological arousal.[15] Let's say you're sitting in a conference room during a meeting. Your colleagues expect you to sit still and pay attention. If your boss says, "Let's take a ten-minute coffee break," everyone will expect you to move around, talk, and engage with others—in other words, you're expected to be more aroused than before. But what if you have trouble shifting between varying states of arousal? When it's time to come back from break and get serious again, you're not going to be able to calm down and sit quietly, and your colleagues will likely see you as disruptive.

Schools have a great deal of trouble handling children who can't easily modify arousal levels. One gym class I observed had fifty students, and the poor gym teacher was trying to manage them all by splitting them into two groups. Half the students were to stay on the bleachers, the other half were to exercise on the gym floor. When the gym teacher blew the whistle, the groups switched. All the kids in the class who had trouble adjusting their arousal levels were supposed to sit quietly on the bleachers, having just engaged in an intense game of dodgeball. They were excited, hyped up, energized. Now they had to be calm. How well do you think that worked out? The gym teacher did the only thing he felt he could do: He sent those kids to the principal's office. Their punishment was to miss recess—the only time they had to work out their restlessness in an appropriate way. Sadly, the students who were deprived of recess were the ones who needed it the most. Everyone in this situation lost—the teacher,

> **The students who were deprived of recess were the ones who needed it the most.**

the kids with poor skills, the other students—all because of an outdated understanding and the interventions that this understanding produced.

EMOTION AND SELF-REGULATION SKILLS

➤ Thinks rationally, even when upset
➤ Manages irritability in an age-appropriate way
➤ Manages anxiety in an age-appropriate way
➤ Manages disappointment in an age-appropriate way
➤ Thinks before responding; considers the likely outcomes or consequences of his/her actions
➤ Can adjust his/her arousal level to meet the demands of a situation (e.g., calming after recess or after getting upset, falling asleep/waking up, staying seated during meetings or meals)

Flexible Thinking Skills: When Learning About Pirates Isn't So Much Fun

Sam exploded into violent tantrums when he became frustrated. On one occasion, he arrived at class to find that the teacher had arranged the desks into the shape of a pirate ship. As the other students entered, the teacher explained that they were about to start a unit on pirates. Most kids were psyched and slid right into their typical morning routine. Sam didn't. He asked what was going on. "We're learning about pirates," the teacher said. "Isn't that exciting?"

"Where's my desk?"

"Don't worry, Sam," the teacher said. "I put your desk right over there in the corner, where you can get to it easily."

Sam shook his head. "That's not my desk."

The teacher smiled. "Yes, it is. It's right there."

"No, it's not."

From here, the encounter degenerated. What happened? It turned out that Sam, like Susan from the last chapter, had deficits in a fourth category of skills, those related to cognitive flexibility, or the ability to adapt his thinking. Most people can easily depart from their preconceived notions. They can think in shades of gray instead of black and white. Some people are much more rigid. They are rule oriented, and they focus on details as opposed to the big picture. They thrive on predictability, routines, and rigid categories and become frustrated when life moves in unexpected or new directions. They are the "need to know" folks, as opposed to the "go with the flow" folks. Sam's desk was no longer in its regular place. So to Sam, it was no longer his desk.

I also call these children "once is always" kids because when they see or hear something one time, they immediately create a template that says it should always go that way. As much as we think our world runs according to clear rules and routines, we live much more in the grays, the exceptions to the rules. Despite clear start and stop times for meetings and clear speed limits for driving, for example, most meetings don't start or end on time and most people exceed the posted speed limit. These minor transgressions drive inflexible thinkers nuts.

Research has revealed links between inflexible thinking and

misbehavior.[16] Autism spectrum disorders and nonverbal learning disabilities are characterized by inflexible thinking, and at least two-thirds of children on the autism spectrum exhibit behavioral difficulties.[17] Yet this doesn't just apply to kids, and you don't need a diagnosis to have a problem. You just need a problem to have a problem! And plenty of people with whom I've worked have struggled with inflexible thinking without receiving a specific diagnosis. It's easy to understand how inflexible thinking can lead to frustration and challenging behavior.

Often, poor flexible thinking skills can result in what Dr. Aaron Beck, creator of cognitive therapy, helped us think of as "stinking thinking." We get ourselves upset when we incorrectly perceive reality. We personalize words or actions, we catastrophize, we overgeneralize, and all this triggers our emotions. You might spill coffee all over yourself one morning. A healthy, productive response might be to think, *Man, this sucks. It's a bad start, but it doesn't mean my whole day will be ruined.* An inflexible thinker has a hard time generating a response like this. Because she thinks in terms of black and white, all or nothing, she gets mired in stinking thinking. *Crap*, this person might say to herself, *my whole day is ruined. This day sucks. I hate my life.* Spilling coffee is just one data point in an entire day, but an inflexible thinker who focuses on details and has a hard time seeing the big picture can't perceive that. Unfortunately, if you perceive that your whole day is ruined right from the start, that impression will likely become a self-fulfilling prophecy.

People with poor flexibility skills get bogged down in all kinds of negative thoughts because of setbacks or challenges they've experienced. Saying the wrong thing to a peer at school and feeling embarrassed becomes: *Oh, my God, everybody hates me, they're all out to get me. I'm stupid.* Doing a bad job on a presentation to the sales team becomes: *I get so nervous. I can't do this. Why am I so nervous? I should be able to speak in front of people like everybody else does.* Some inflexible thinkers also develop "sticky thinking," getting stuck on a thought, desire, plan, or want. Nothing can shake an idea out of their heads. They become obsessed and perseverate. Challenging behavior follows in due course.

FLEXIBLE THINKING SKILLS

- ➤ Handles transitions; shifts easily from one task to another
- ➤ Is able to see shades of gray rather than thinking only in black and white
- ➤ Thinks hypothetically; is able to envision different possibilities
- ➤ Handles deviations from rules, routines, and original plans
- ➤ Handles unpredictability, ambiguity, uncertainty, and novelty
- ➤ Can shift away from an original idea, solution, or plan
- ➤ Takes into account situational factors that may mean a change in plans (e.g., "If it rains, we may need to cancel")
- ➤ Interprets information accurately/avoids overgeneralizing or personalizing (e.g., avoids saying "Everyone's out to get me," "Nobody likes me," "You always blame me," "It's not fair," "I'm stupid," or "Things will never work out for me")

Social Thinking Skills: Why Jeff in Accounting Tells Too Many Jokes

One child I worked with was obsessed with Pokémon cards. He would barge into my office and ask, "Do you want to play Pokémon?" He wouldn't bother to take stock of what was going on around him. If he had, he would have questioned whether it was an appropriate time to play Pokémon. If I agreed to play Pokémon, he would drop to the floor and unpack all of his cards. Motioning for me to get down on the floor next to him, he would go about an obsessive exercise playing Pokémon, in essence, by himself. I could go to lunch and return forty-five minutes later, and he would still be playing, unaware of my absence.

This child had trouble with a final category of skills, called social thinking skills. While struggling with pretty much any of the skills discussed above can cause trouble in social situations (think of how working memory skills allow you to hold your own in a conversation), there are still social thinking skills that we need specifically in order to behave appropriately in interactions with others.[18] Some of these are basic skills such as knowing how to start a conversation with someone, how to make eye contact, how to gauge whether someone is interested in what you're saying, how to greet someone, and so on. People lacking in these skills can struggle to perform tasks that most of us take for granted: sharing, entering a group, starting a conversation, taking turns in a conversation, recognizing boredom when speaking with someone, and regulating pitch and volume.

The lack of these basic social thinking skills can give rise to behavior that seems disruptive, unpleasant, or hostile.[19] I once worked with a correctional facility inmate named Jimmy who got along well with a particular guard. Yet every day when the guards changed shifts and this guard arrived, Jimmy greeted him by screaming, "Hey, you motherfucker! Good to see you, you fucking bastard!" The guard was perplexed. He and Jimmy seemed to have a great relationship. Jimmy always came to see him whenever he had a problem. We discovered that Jimmy struggled with the skill of saying hello to people, which is more complicated than first meets the eye. We're all expected to greet people differently depending on the social context. Most of us have no trouble assessing the context and adjusting our speech or actions in an appropriate way. For some of us, that skill doesn't come naturally. Jimmy didn't understand how to greet the guard in a friendly way when he was glad to see him without causing his fellow inmates to resent him and beat the crap out of him for cozying up to a guard. This more nuanced social interaction was beyond Jimmy.

Other, more complicated social thinking skills that bedevil some people include what psychologists call perspective taking. Interacting well with others requires being able to understand how your behavior impacts others and how others perceive you, and it also requires you to appreciate someone else's perspective, especially if it differs from yours. All of this in turn requires a capacity to read and understand other people's emotions. Humans, in effect, largely depend on a feedback loop to get along in the world. We speak and act, and we then scan the environment to see how people view us. We also read and interpret the signals coming back to us. Based on that feedback, we might adjust our speech and conduct to align them better with our desired goals.

This feedback loop can break down in all kinds of ways. Some people lack a functioning loop and do not receive *any* data on what others are thinking. They come across as cold and distant because they behave in ways that make it *seem* like they don't care about others. These individuals might very well be warm and empathic—if only they were receiving data about others' perceptions and could understand it.

Remember the adolescent I worked with who said he didn't know what he was thinking until he said it out loud? Beyond poor impulse control, this teenager had deficits in social thinking that caused his feedback loop to remain activated for only very brief periods of time. DeJaun was witty and would blurt out jokes in the middle of class. When other kids laughed, DeJaun would stand up and start delivering a monologue. The teacher found this horribly disruptive, as did the other kids after a while. They would turn their backs, make faces at DeJaun, and tell him to knock it off. But DeJaun didn't know *how* to knock it off because his social feedback loop was operating for only that initial moment during which he saw the kids (and the teacher!) laughing. He shut down his feedback loop after a few seconds and stopped collecting data, so he couldn't read how he was coming across, and he couldn't accurately interpret incoming feedback from others as he was talking. He was convinced that others in the room were continuing to respond well to his continued jokes, even though they weren't. The DeJauns of the world are often described as not knowing when enough is enough. How would you know when enough is enough? Because your feedback loop tells you!

SOCIAL THINKING SKILLS

➤ Pays attention to verbal and nonverbal social cues

➤ Accurately interprets nonverbal social cues (like facial expressions and tone of voice)

➤ Starts conversations with peers; enters groups of peers appropriately

➤ Seeks attention in appropriate ways

➤ Understands how his/her behavior affects other people

➤ Understands how he/she is coming across or being perceived by others

➤ Empathizes with others; appreciates others' perspectives or points of view

Charting the Deficits

Is it nature or nurture? The answer is yes.

You might wonder why some people struggle with neurocognitive skills and others don't. What causes skills deficits? Is it nature or nurture? The answer is yes. From research, it seems clear that genetics play a role, but so do environmental factors—most notably chronic stress during childhood. When children experience trauma such as domestic abuse, sexual or physical abuse, or the chronic stress of poverty, the impact can be toxic and delay brain development.[20] This in turn causes skill delays. Chronic, toxic stress can cause biological differences in brain formation that are visible in imaging scans of the brain.[21] Compare a scan of a neurotypically developed toddler's brain with one of the brain of a toddler who has been deprived, and you'll see a striking difference. The neurotypical toddler's brain shows activity in the prefrontal cortex, which is responsible for many of the higher-order thinking skills I've been discussing. The brain scan of a deprived toddler is depressingly dark in these areas.

My friend and colleague Dr. Bruce Perry, senior fellow at the Child Trauma Academy in Houston, Texas, is one of the leading experts on the impact of childhood trauma on brain development.[22] As he has argued, children confronted with chronic stress adapt to their environments by activating their fight-or-flight response. They use more primitive, lower parts of their brain—the brain stem and amygdala to respond to even non-threatening events. Over time, they are primed to go directly to fight-or-flight when confronted by outside stimulation. They're in a heightened state of arousal, ever vigilant and fearful, ready to meet a threat. Information often never reaches the part of the brain associated with higher-order cognitive functioning, the prefrontal cortex. As a result, these children can't build and access neurocognitive skills the ways normal children do. As Perry writes, "A child with a brain adapted for an environment of chaos, unpredictability, threat, and distress is ill-suited to the modern playground or classroom."[23] Later in life, they're often unsuited to the modern workplace or university and have difficulty maintaining stable, healthy relationships.

Don't make the mistake of thinking that this type of trauma is rare, however. The Adverse Childhood Experiences (ACE) study[24] surveyed more than seventeen thousand HMO members about their histories of experiences like physical and emotional abuse and neglect; witnessing domestic violence, parental separation or divorce; and having a parent with mental illness, substance abuse problems, or in jail. About two-thirds of the people surveyed reported at least one such adverse childhood experience, and 87 percent of people who reported one also reported at least one additional adverse childhood experience. And indeed, the study found that the more of these adverse childhood experiences you have, the more health, social, and behavioral problems you will have throughout your life as well.

While trauma and toxic stress are pretty surefire ways to arrest brain development and cause difficulties with certain skills, delays in brain development can also arise from other causes. Anyone can struggle with certain skills, either lacking them entirely or experiencing developmental delays or weaknesses. All of us are stronger in some cognitive areas and weaker in others, although most of us may not be so weak in any one skill that we experience significant trouble functioning. People with chronic stress, however, are more likely to experience significant skills deficits that prevent them from behaving as others might expect, or from behaving "adaptively," as psychologists say, to handle new situations as they arise.

How authority figures treat people with skills deficits can magnify the behavioral effects of these deficits. Parents, managers, and partners can have their own skills deficits that affect how they respond to skills deficits in others. Depending on one person's own areas of weaknesses, they can behave in ways that combine with the weaknesses of another person to make behavior worse.[25] For instance, when both a parent and a child struggle with flexible thinking, disputes can easily flare up and burn out of control. When both a manager and a direct report struggle with perspective taking, misunderstandings and empathic failures can make their working relationship untenable. Each party inadvertently pushes against the other's needs. Similar dynamics can of course also occur among romantic partners and people in any other kind of relationship.

What Getting up to Go to Work *Really* Entails

Again, it may seem puzzling that cognitive scientists know so much about these skills, yet people and institutions still regard behavior almost exclusively as a matter of will and intention. This gap between science and everyday practice is even more striking given how *intuitively* correct the notion of *skill, not will* is. In my presentations, I ask people in the room to describe something they didn't want to do but did anyway. Someone will invariably chime in, "Getting up at six a.m. on a cold, rainy day to go to work when I totally didn't feel like it."

Okay, I'll ask, so why did you do it?

"Because I didn't want to lose my job," the person will say.

Although at first glance this seems like a simple attempt to avoid punishment, I'll point out to the group that this is a prime example of impulse control—a person not wanting to go to work, but resisting the impulse to stay in bed and getting up at six a.m. anyway. The decision to go to work under these circumstances also involves the skill of projecting into the future and gauging the likely effects of your actions, being fired—an executive function skill called forecasting.

Another person might say, "So often I'm feeling nice and comfy in bed, but I just push myself through it, get up, and get myself moving."

I observe that this person was deploying her self-regulation skills. She had to adjust her arousal level, moving from "sleeping and dead to the world" to "up and about."

Someone else might say, "I get up by psyching myself to do it. I think to myself that once I get up, I'll turn on a nice hot shower, which always wakes me up." I point out that this person is not only thinking ahead, but thinking in more nuanced, flexible ways. Instead of adopting an all-or-nothing approach and catastrophizing the situation ("This day totally sucks. It's raining. This will be the worst day ever!"), this person is acknowledging the challenge of a rainy day, but also recognizing that the next twenty-four hours are not predestined to be awful—there is a hot shower that can turn the day around.

In all of these cases, the individuals involved are also using language and communication skills to solve problems. They're talking the problems through in their heads in order to arrive at solutions that allow them to behave adaptively and get out of bed.

Thus, choosing to get out of bed, or failing to do so, isn't primarily a matter of will. What we think of as will actually requires the mobilization of specific abilities that fall under our five skills categories. All day long, every minute of the day, we're deploying cognitive skills in order to function in the world, the vast majority of the time unknowingly. And if you lack skills in one or more of those areas, or if you're weak in them, you might *not* get out of bed, and you'll suffer the consequences. You'll behave in all kinds of ways that others around you might find disruptive, distasteful, unhelpful, illegal, or just plain wrong.

The way to address bad behavior isn't to punish it. It's to build skills. And that's the best news of all. We *can* improve a person's skills or even build them up from scratch, no matter if their weakness owes to genetics, chronic stress, or anything else. Everyone's behavior is changeable as long as you think *skill, not will.* In the process, we can actualize and enhance the growth mind-set that, as Dr. Carol Dweck has argued, is so favorable for improving behavior and performance.[26] Later in this book, I'll present a simple method for addressing behavior problems via skill building that tens of thousands of people have already applied with impressive results. First, let's understand the opportunity that reforming discipline represents. By ignoring what decades of science has shown to be true, we're wasting billions of dollars and causing untold emotional pain. If we can fix how we handle behavior problems, we'll improve the performance of institutions and businesses while also helping to build a safer, healthier, more compassionate society.

> The way to address bad behavior isn't to punish it. It's to build skills.

CHAPTER THREE

Discipline Gone Awry

At a workshop I led in 2015, an audience member raised his hand and asked to speak. He was in his midfifties, a demure, professorial type. From the intensity of his gaze and his faltering tone, he seemed upset. I wondered why. I had been talking about "willpower" and the failings of traditional discipline, and the conversation until that point hadn't been especially emotional.

"I'm the parent of a seventeen-year-old," he said, "and while I'm glad to be here, I feel so awful. I can see now that I've been misunderstanding my kid all these years."

I tried to reassure him, telling him that it was okay. None of us is a perfect parent.

"No, you don't understand," he said, his mouth quivering with anguish. "Now that I know what was really causing his bad behavior, I realize that I've been making his life miserable for years by continuing to punish him and just making him feel worse about himself. *For years.*" He shook his head, ashen faced, and stared at the floor.

"Well, you can always start now," I offered.

He sighed and shook his head. "I don't know. I think it may be too late." He paused for a moment, holding back tears. "I may have ruined him."

I didn't agree that this father had "ruined" his son by disciplining him in conventional ways. But the core of what he was saying was correct. Traditional discipline does tremendous damage to kids on the receiving end. Think of the years of pain this man's son must have endured when hit with punishment after punishment, even when he was doing his best. Millions of kids are paying a terrible price because we've ignored the science of challenging behavior. But it's not just our kids. It's our partners, our families, our institutions, and society as a whole. We wonder why American institutions are under strain, why workers in both the public and the private sectors are unhappy and stressed out, why there's never enough money in government budgets. Such dysfunction has many causes, but one of the biggest—conventional discipline—has gone unremarked. As even a rough and extremely partial accounting suggests, traditional rewards and punishments are wasting tens of billions of dollars, maybe more. A huge opportunity exists to improve society by revamping how we respond when people behave in challenging ways. Before examining the costs to public institutions and private businesses, let's spend a little more time understanding the human costs to kids and their families.

"I Wish We'd Never Had Him"

What would you do if your child, that little bundle of joy you brought home from the hospital, began behaving like a monster? Bob and Marlene Booker can tell you what that's like. They noticed behavior issues in their son Jamison when he was only two and a half years old. Jealous of his baby brother, Charles, he clawed at the baby's face until it bled, and he also acted out by throwing temper tantrums and destroying his favorite toys.

As Jamison grew older, he became more aggressive, ranting and raving when things didn't go his way, flying into violent rages at seemingly minor requests from his parents. "He absolutely refuses to wear his glasses," Marlene told me. "He has broken more than thirty pairs. He'll look at me and say 'fuck you' and snap them in half." Age thirteen as of this writing, he has broken everything in the family's house, including two flat-screen TVs, countless cell phones, and a glass door on the stove. He has stolen money, kicked holes in walls, and vandalized the house with spray paint. On one occasion, his grandmother was so upset by his behavior that she called him a monster to his face.

The Bookers haven't taken Jamison's behavior lightly. Early on, they levied the usual punishments, sending him to time-out or rewarding him for good behavior. These techniques failed. "Whenever we tried rewards or time-outs, it was like we were speaking a foreign language," Marlene said. "Never once did he sit still in a time-out. Never once did he willingly go to his room. And if we got him there, he would destroy his room, he was so angry. We would open the door and it would be like a war zone."

Desperate for a solution, the Bookers brought their son to a therapist, starting at age three. It didn't work. During the years that followed, the family tried psychiatrists, psychologists, hospitalization—every variety of expert, most of them advocating some form of conventional rewards and punishments. None of it helped. As Marlene remembered, "He was beyond any therapist's pay grade. He never did anything any of them ever said. He just wouldn't cooperate." With each therapist, Jamison's behavior got only more terrifying and out of control. He would fly into violent rages four or five times a week. He wouldn't brush his teeth, wouldn't eat healthy food, wouldn't do *anything* his parents wanted him to. He was completely unmanageable.

The constant, chronic behavior issues traumatized the entire Booker family. Bob and Marlene blamed themselves for the situation, wondering what they had done wrong. Marlene became anxious and depressed and had to go on medication. She felt depleted from the constant struggle of dealing with Jamison's flare-ups, so much so that she had to quit her job to keep things running at home. "I haven't worked," she says, "because I didn't have the bandwidth to sit in a meeting after an episode with Jamison when he's attacked us or he's been in a hospital. I couldn't be a professional mom pretending everything is fine in my life and come home and there is a war zone." The whole experience was "exhausting, beyond anything else, the most exhausting thing in the world. And there's no escape with a child like this. No pause button, no going away for the weekend for a mini break."

With all the tumult at home, Marlene's social life has become nonexistent. She's too tired to go out for a drink or to dinner with her friends. Even going on a walk with a friend is tough, because the only thing she has to talk about is her son, and she doesn't want "to be a Debbie Downer."

The Bookers' marriage has come under severe strain. Marlene had been the family's main breadwinner, so her inability to work has left the family struggling. With every spare cent going toward Jamison's treatment, vacations are out of the question, and they have to ask family members for help. When Bob comes home from work, he and Marlene don't enjoy relaxed time together. There's always conflict flaring up, or consequences of prior conflicts they must address. The two also don't always agree on how to handle Jamison's behavior. Since Marlene has been home with the kids, she has felt the full brunt of Jamison's challenging behavior, and she is more inclined to crack down. Bob can let things slide, because he comes home and enjoys more quality time with the boys, who are thrilled to see him.

The couple can't even go out for dinner by themselves without worrying about what Jamison might do. On one occasion while they were out, he became so furious at their absence that he escaped from the house without the babysitter's knowledge and walked over to the restaurant in search of them. The babysitter was so upset that he wouldn't work for them for a year.

All of the turbulence at home has taken a toll on Jamison's little brother. Charles has taken years of abuse from his brother, having been hit, punched, and kicked. After all that, Marlene reports, "Charles has no interest in having anything to do with Jamison." He has been embarrassed socially by Jamison, having to figure out how to explain to his friends that his brother was in a psychiatric hospital.

Marlene summed up the family's life in the bleakest of terms. She said it was a "living hell," and although she knew it was terrible to say, she found herself "wanting to kill Jamison" at times. "In the aftermath of his meltdowns, I can't help but wish that we never had him. I think: *Oh, my God, how can we live through this?* I tell my husband, 'I just fucking hate him.' He has ruined our lives and is still ruining our lives. He's the reason our lives are difficult."

Leo Tolstoy famously observed in the first line of his novel *Anna Karenina* that "[a]ll happy families are alike; each unhappy family is unhappy in its own way."[1] Whether or not you subscribe to that theory, one thing is true: In so many unhappy families, conventional rewards and punishments actually *increase* the amount of suffering and unhappiness. I've seen evidence of this not just in the Bookers' story, but in hundreds of cases that have come through my clinical practice. Observing this dynamic in kids and families helps us understand how it applies in so many other settings and with people of all ages as well.

> In so many unhappy families, conventional rewards and punishments actually *increase* the amount of suffering and unhappiness.

When children in these families misbehave, parents usually remove some sort of privilege or levy a punishment. They take away an allowance or Xbox privileges. They don't let children go on playdates. Such measures don't address the underlying skills deficits that produced the challenging behavior. Instead, they aggravate or upset a child, *escalating* the bad behavior. Even the threat of imposing a punishment or removing a privilege can cause children to become more aggressive or defiant. And as their behavior escalates, parents become more frustrated. They up the ante, levying even harsher consequences. This dynamic creates an environment of chronic conflict in the home, in some cases pushing parents to the breaking point. Parents become so upset that they lash out. Alternately, they give up the fight, shaking their heads at a situation they feel powerless to resolve.

The damage traditional discipline causes to the parent–child relationship is bad enough, but as the Bookers' story suggests, this is just the beginning. Challenging behavior puts the entire family system under strain, including the siblings of kids with behavioral problems. When one child acts out and parents respond in traditional ways, they often wind up devoting many of the family's emotional and financial resources to solving that problem. Siblings with better skills feel pressure to behave as "model" children to help keep the family functioning. They often feel ignored, as if the whole family revolves around the challenging kid and their needs are a lesser priority. When conflict arises, they let their challenging brother or sister have his or her way in the moment.

Over time, siblings become angry and resentful, but it's hard for them to articulate these emotions. They wind up carrying the emotions around with them, often unknowingly. As I've seen in my clinical practice, these kids go on to experience problems with anxiety, depression, eating disorders, and the like, and these problems often persist into adulthood. Their parents feel guilty for having failed to prevent these problems. As I tell parents, it's not their fault. They were handling the challenging behavior the best way they could, and in line with what conventional wisdom believes to be true. But, unbeknownst to them, traditional discipline was doomed to fail.

In addition to siblings, parents suffer many personal consequences thanks to the failure of conventional discipline. I've seen many instances where parents have had to quit their jobs or downshift their careers in order to deal with chronic misbehavior that, despite the application of rewards and punishments, never improves. Like the Bookers, these are some of the most well-meaning parents in the world, yet they are unknowing victims of traditional thinking that is misguided and ineffective. We must do better for these people and their kids. The impact of rewards and punishments on families is simply too damaging.

On Track to Fail

The costs of traditional discipline are just as serious in schools and other institutions serving children as they are in families. The vast majority of children—as many as 90 percent—adapt fairly well to school. The remainder, those so-called disruptive kids, come into regular or sustained contact with school disciplinary systems. When children misbehave at school, the problems usually start at a very early age—in kindergarten, even in pre-school. Instead of addressing the underlying skills deficits at that point, teachers are taught to apply rewards and punishments.

Just as in the home, the problems worsen. Soon these "problem children" are expelled from preschool, not just once, but over and over again. The number of children expelled from preschool each year is astounding.[2]

As these children grow older, they continue to receive the usual school punishments—detention, suspension, and expulsion. Schools create Individualized Education Programs (IEPs) for them, allocating special resources to help with their behavioral issues. They assign aides to work with these children or move them into self-contained classrooms designed specifically for kids with behavioral difficulties. IEPs contain behavior remediation plans, but these plans don't necessarily—and usually don't— address the underlying skills. Usually the plan just tries to improve the kid's motivation by making use of a system of rewards and punishments, like a sticker chart or a level system. In other words, children typically experience the same basic forms of discipline they have in the past, only more stringently and with closer monitoring. Over time, these children become angry and alienated from school. This is entirely understandable. They've been removed from the community again and again, treated as offenders for behavior lapses that they cannot easily control. They would change if they were able. But they aren't.

When these alternative arrangements fail, as they frequently do, schools place children in special therapeutic schools and residential treatment facilities. I wish the journey of a challenging kid ended there, but it doesn't. As I've noted, children with behavioral difficulties often commit crimes, winding up in the juvenile correctional system. A big part of the problem is precisely the discipline applied. If the usual rewards and punishments worked, we would expect to see fewer of them as time went on. Yet many districts are seeing *more* suspensions. Between 1974 and 2006, the number of school suspensions in the United States *doubled*, largely because of harsh zero tolerance policies.[3] That's tragic: Academic studies have documented a connection between suspensions from school, for instance, and academic deterioration, premature dropout, and increased risk of criminal activity and incarceration, fueling the school-to-prison pipeline.[4] As challenging children become adults, they commit more crimes and "graduate" into the adult correctional system.

Think of the harm this pipeline imposes. Millions of children in our country wind up going down the wrong path in life, pushed along by school disciplinary systems that don't work. Yet the cost isn't just borne by these kids. When kids chronically misbehave at school, they disrupt learning for their well-behaved peers, and they dramatically increase the burden on teachers. Disruptive behavior is the number-one source of teacher stress and the number-one predictor of early teacher dropout in the United States.[5] Many talented teachers find themselves so frustrated and exhausted by chronic challenging behavior that they leave their jobs and find work in other fields.[6]

A look at one teacher's story illustrates the point. At the age of twenty-three, Sam earned her master's degree in teaching and went to teach social studies at a charter school in New York City's South Bronx. "I was handed a textbook and a bunch of kids," she recalls, "and it became very clear that I had to manage behavior in my own classroom because I couldn't really depend on the administration."[7] From the first day, Sam encountered frequent misbehavior, including cursing, talking back to the teacher, arguing and physical altercations between the kids, and the disruptive use of cell phones. Not knowing what else to do, she started kicking disruptive kids out of her classroom, sending them to the principal's office. The kids kept coming back, their behavioral issues even worse. "I probably cried every single day that first year," she recalls. "I hated it, hated it, hated it."

Over the next five years, Sam taught at other tough New York City schools. In addition to the same daily behavioral issues, she had a number of physical altercations with students. On one occasion, an angry child threw his desk and chair clear across the classroom. On another occasion, she had to break up a fight between two boys who were both much bigger than she was. On still another, she had to separate two girls who were bitterly arguing and pulling out each other's hair. The worst were episodes when Sam felt threatened by groups of students, or when she had to walk alone after dark from the school to the subway fearing some kind of retribution.

Fortunately, Sam was never the victim of violence. With time, she got better at controlling her classroom, and she came to enjoy teaching more. Weekly therapy appointments helped her process some of what she was seeing. Still, it was never easy, and part of the stress accrued from having to pay so much attention to developing the perfect lesson plan. With so much misbehavior, she felt pressure to keep the kids constantly entertained so that they would stay calm and learn. "It felt like every single day, all day long, I needed to be on and excited and smiley," she says. During the evenings, she came home, lit a candle, and just lay on her couch under a blanket, trying to recover. She didn't have the strength to do anything else.

As hard as her life was, some of her colleagues fared worse. They had complete breakdowns, leaving school one day never to return. When that happened, Sam remarks, it was "just a huge loss to these kids. Then they have subs for two months, and then the school hires another teacher who is coming into a lose-lose situation."

Eventually, the behavioral issues became too much for Sam as well. Although she had come to love the kids and sought to help them, she wanted a family of her own, and it didn't seem possible to teach in such a difficult environment and still enjoy a normal, healthy life at home. All her colleagues felt the same way. At the last school where she taught, only one out of approximately eighty staff members had children. During the time she spent at the school, she saw some twenty-five teachers quit their jobs, either because they couldn't handle the stress or because they saw it as precluding a healthy family life.

Challenging behavior doesn't just impact individual teachers. It brings down entire schools. One principal at a middle and high school in Brooklyn, New York, recalled how her school struggled for years with "a small percentage of students whose behavior we could neither control nor understand." With only traditional discipline to fall back on, the school did the best it could: "Our reaction was always to hold our breath just a little until we could tell if this was a good day or a bad day. . . . Every meltdown, every escalation, every suspension, left us feeling defeated and unsuccessful."[8] Like staff at so many schools, her faculty members felt like they were being held hostage by challenging behavior. With so much disciplining going on, much less time and energy remained for teaching and learning. Everyone lost.

Discipline and Punish—and Pay

So far, we've discussed only the human costs of conventional discipline. The economic costs are staggering as well. Even if only 10 percent of students experience behavioral problems, that's still millions of kids. It costs a typical school district at least $40,000 a year to provide special out-of-district services for a single student with chronic challenging behavior. Perhaps 15 to 20 percent of "problem" students will need these services no matter what system of discipline exists (kids with severe psychiatric issues, for instance). But the vast majority of these students might be helped if we only found ways to address their underlying skills deficits. That amounts to billions of dollars spent every year on discipline that doesn't work. Consider, too, the cost of recruiting and hiring new teachers when existing teachers leave, or the cost of keeping tens of thousands of school safety officers and police officers stationed at schools (New York City alone has more than fifty-five hundred school safety officers and agents in its schools, which, if it were to stand on its own, would comprise the third-largest police force in the United States).

The economic costs of traditional discipline run up and down the school-to-prison pipeline, at every institution that touches challenging kids during their childhoods and when they mature into adults. The behavior of some of these children result in inpatient stays in psychiatric hospitals, and psychiatric institutions spend thousands of dollars on medications and physical restraints for each unruly inpatient.[9] The act of restraining patients often results in injuries to patient and staff, and on occasion it has led to death. For this reason, state governments have stepped in to try to reduce the frequency with which organizations use restraints. The potential cost savings is enormous. One midsized organization we studied had to restrain patients 1,300 times a year, at an estimated cost of $350 per incident in addition to staff time. Imagine what would happen if we could reduce that number by one thousand incidents per year by treating behavioral challenges as a lack of skill, not a lack of will. That one organization would save $350,000 per year. Actually, they did save that much. By transforming the disciplinary strategies at this organization, we reduced the number of restraints by one thousand a year. Similar reductions across our system nationwide would again result in billions of dollars in cost savings.[10]

One published study has considered in detail how much it cost a small (thirty-bed) inpatient facility in Westborough, Massachusetts, to apply restraints on patients, and how much it saved when it complied with a state initiative to reduce the use of restraints. The study considered the time staff spent on each episode when it restrained out-of-control patients as well as the cost of the medication used. It didn't factor in costs from related expenses, such as injuries to staff and turnover, nor did it attempt to quantify costs related to the need to monitor patients after an incident in which restraints were used.

The study found that this organization reduced the number of episodes in which staff restrained patients from 3,991 to 373 episodes over a three-year period. That represented a total cost savings of more than $1 million on an annual basis. Recidivism among patients plummeted, while turnover among the staff decreased by 80 percent. The number of staff workdays missed due to injury declined by 98 percent, with workers' compensation claims declining by 29 percent and medical costs due to injury declining by 98 percent.[11]

At detention centers and prisons, the costs of traditional discipline are no less great. Recidivism is a huge problem for our criminal justice system. According to a Pew Center study, close to 50 percent of offenders returned to prison within three years of their release. Despite dramatic increases in prison budgets (as of 2011, our country spent some $52 billion on prisons), recidivism rates have barely declined.[12] A study by the Department of Justice found that 75 percent of prisoners would be back in handcuffs "within five years of their release."[13] Such recidivism represents a damning indictment of conventional discipline. Prison is supposed to rehabilitate people. That inmates keep returning suggests that the rewards and punishments used there are not addressing inmates' underlying skills deficits.

In the confines of a prison or a juvenile detention center, it might seem perfectly fine to use rewards and punishments, and not worry about skills. When inmates misbehave, you can immediately subdue them and, in extreme situations, lock them down in their cells. You might think that you're "teaching the inmate a lesson," giving him a strong incentive never to behave poorly. His bad behavior is "corrected." But what happens when that inmate gets out of prison? Nobody is following him around with handcuffs, ready to lock him down. He still has the same skills deficits that brought him into the prison in the first place, and he isn't able to respond any more adaptively to problems that arise, no matter how much motivation he may have to remain free. The criminal justice system becomes a revolving door, to the point where some correctional system administrators I've talked to joke grimly about it. "Good-bye," they say to inmates, "see you soon." They know they probably will, unfortunately.

According to a 2012 study of forty states, the total cost of prisons was $39 billion, with an average cost of more than $31,000 per inmate per year.[14] If we could reduce recidivism by just 10 percent by reforming the traditional approaches to discipline that almost all prisons use, we could save billions of dollars. And we have every reason to think that we could cut recidivism by far more than 10 percent. In one institution that I'll discuss later, we were able to reduce recidivism by *50 percent* over five years by applying an alternative to conventional discipline.

Massive Societal Ramifications

In addition to individual human costs, conventional discipline exacts broader costs to society, directly affecting us all. The workplace is an important example. Most businesses apply rewards and punishments to encourage desired behavior (for example, faster or more efficient performance) and discourage undesirable behavior (for example, conducting personal business during work hours). Seldom do organizations take steps to remedy underlying skills deficits among their employees. Challenging behavior persists or worsens, leading to chronic conflict among team members and an impoverished work environment.

A clear casualty of chronic conflict is performance. As I mentioned in this book's introduction, I define challenging behavior broadly as either behavior we don't like or the failure to behave in ways we *do* like. In the workplace, a subset of challenging behavior is "uncivil" behavior—nasty speech, body language, and other instances of rudeness. As one survey of eight hundred workers found, 48 percent "intentionally decreased their work effort" when hit by incivility, while a similar percentage spent less time at work and two-thirds reported that their performance suffered. Managers are hardly spared, as they're the ones who must react when people behave rudely. One study found that managers and executives at large companies spent seven weeks out of the year "mending employee relationships and otherwise dealing with the aftermath of incivility."[15] As you can guess, managers seldom solve these problems through attempts at skill building.

Any attempt to calculate the economic costs of challenging behavior to businesses quickly produces some big numbers. The eight-hundred-worker survey mentioned above also found that the vast majority (78 percent) of respondents subject to rudeness at work "said their commitment to the organization declined," almost half "intentionally decreased the time spent at work," and over 10 percent "said they had left their job because of the uncivil treatment."[16] Extended across the economy, these numbers would suggest a potential loss of billions of dollars in the form of reduced productivity and employee attrition. In addition, we must factor in the billions of dollars lost when employees who experience bad behavior at work become unmotivated, disengaged, and stressed out, and the billions of dollars that arise from the health impact of stress due to incivility (workplace stress from all causes costs society up to $190 billion in health care costs each year).[17]

Even these big numbers likely understate the toll taken by

challenging behavior. In their 2009 book about incivility in the workplace, Christine Pearson and Christine Porath write that

> [i]ncivility's true impact stretches far beyond that which is measurable in dollar terms. How to tally damage done by increased employee turnover, by the disruption of work teams, by the waning of helpful behavior, or by the tarnishing of corporate or individual reputations? . . . Far from a minor inconvenience to millions of American workers, workplace incivility is one of today's most substantial economic drains on American business, a largely preventable ill that begs to be addressed.[18]

Remember that uncivil behavior is but a subset of the challenging behavior I'm describing. Colleagues can behave in ways that are overtly civil but still bother others and create conflict. They can become overwhelmed, forget about meetings, and struggle to meet deadlines, or they can fail to pick up on basic social cues and behave awkwardly (but not rudely or offensively). The true cost of challenging behavior is likely to surpass even that of incivility in the workplace. By failing to deal with challenging behavior and by instead helping to generate even more of it, conventional discipline makes this ill much worse than it needs to be.

Looking beyond the workplace, conventional discipline corrodes social relationships and civil discourse generally. Systems of rewards and punishments define our lives from earliest childhood through adulthood, shaping how we behave and think. We become accustomed to perceiving bad behavior as a product of willful action on the part of the offender. When a person offends, we want to punish and reassert our will. We're not used to spending time trying to understand the offender's point of view or the underlying causes of his behavior. Whether it's parents with their children, teachers with students, managers with staff, society trying to deal with criminals, or governments trying to deal with rogue states, an attitude of *might makes right* takes hold. We possess the ability to reward and punish, and we go about blindly asserting *our* will. Bigger, more powerful people or groups dictate solutions, teaching less powerful ones "a lesson" so that their behavior will conform.

> *Might makes right* is almost never the best way to resolve a conflict.

In any context, *might makes right* is almost never the best way to resolve a conflict. People and groups on the receiving end of rewards and punishments feel disenfranchised. With so many "lessons" being meted out, they feel unheard and powerless. While they may look like they are conforming, anger and resentment mount beneath the surface. The results play out in the roiling tensions and violence we read about every day: school shootings, disillusioned extremists committing terrorist acts, military conflict between nations that bear grievances toward one another. My point is not to deny or diminish the sympathy we should all feel toward the victims of challenging behavior. When a murderer strikes, when a country invades another country, when a bully acts out—it's wrong, and it hurts. But by rushing to punish offending countries, groups, and individuals, we're failing to listen to them, and to understand what led to their acting out. We're not getting at the root causes of behavior we don't like, which is what we will need to do in order to fix it, and we're sowing the seeds for more bad behavior in the future. We're eroding the social ties that underpin civil society at every level.

We're also reinforcing for the next generation the notion that people behave badly because they want to, and that the way to resolve disputes is to impose our will. The next time your child acts out, think about your reaction. If you lash out and levy a punishment, you're teaching your child that this is how people in positions of authority should behave when confronted with a problem. Your punishment probably won't solve the behavior issue. What it will do is teach your children that when they grow up and get bigger and stronger they will finally have a chance to impose their will on others, unless they can find less powerful people in the meantime.

Enough of Plan A

My intention here is not to make people in positions of authority feel bad about themselves. It's to convince them to try something different, something more effective. As my colleagues and I have found, people of any age are changeable by eschewing old, counterproductive systems of rewards and punishments and focusing instead on building their underlying skills. We've taken hardened seventeen-year-old kids who have been in and out of correctional facilities for years and dramatically improved their behavior by working on their skills. In entire prisons and psychiatric hospitals, we've dramatically reduced recidivism rates while doing away with the need for interventions like restraints or isolation rooms.

Parents, teachers, colleagues, police officers, business leaders, and political leaders have all done the best that they could with the disciplinary tools at their disposal. They've tried what we might call Plan A. It's time to try something new, something radically different that has actually been shown to work. It's time to try Plan B.

CHAPTER FOUR

Plan B

Tell me and I forget, teach me and I may remember,
involve me and I learn.

—BEN FRANKLIN

A student at one of the country's toughest high schools has a run-in with a uniformed school security agent at the school. The girl has left school grounds but has returned, having realized that she left her subway pass in her locker. The security agent refuses to let her back in, because that's against regulations (the school has this rule to make it harder for kids to bring prohibited items with them back into the school). The girl becomes enraged. "This is stupid. Let me the fuck in. I'm getting my pass." The agent tells the girl not to speak to him that way. "Well, fuck you," the girl says. "Who the fuck are you? You're just a fucking fake cop." The security agent doesn't put up with this. He tells her she'd better stand down, because he isn't letting her through. She tries to push past him anyway, and when he grabs hold of her, she throws an elbow at him. The officer calls for backup and arrests her for assault. She is led away in handcuffs.

Scenarios like this one unfold every day in school districts around the country. School resource officers must navigate extremely challenging situations with volatile students, and they receive little training in how to do so. As a result, students are arrested and channeled through the school-to-prison pipeline. Officers do the best they can, but let's consider a different way we could have trained the officer to respond. First, he could have calmed the student by empathizing with her situation and reassuring her of his intention to help. Despite her harsh language, he might have said, "I get it. You just walked out and forgot your pass. Anyone could make that mistake. And now you need it to get to where you're going. Don't worry, I want to help. Okay? We can figure this out." From here, the officer could have expressed his own set of concerns: "Here's where I'm stuck. I'm not allowed to let people in. There are rules, and if I bend them for you, I could lose my job." Perhaps the student would have gotten upset again, but the officer could have calmed her by saying something like: "I know we can figure this out. I really want to help you get your pass." Afterward, he might have worked with the student to collaboratively investigate possible solutions. "What can we do to get you your bus pass *without* me breaking the rules. Any ideas?"

After a certain amount of back-and-forth, the officer and the student might have decided on a solution together. This might have been an innovative arrangement that satisfied both parties but required that neither compromise. For instance, a friend still inside the school could have retrieved the bus pass and brought it down to the girl. Or another agent could have retrieved it for her.

If the officer had responded in this way, both he and the girl would have addressed their respective concerns. The officer would have been doing his job, maintaining his authority and the integrity of the rules. The girl would have gotten her pass and would not have gotten arrested, avoiding the trauma and embarrassment that come with that and the increased chance of winding up in the correctional system. Instead, she would have built a relationship with the agent. And as we'll see, she would have had a chance to practice skills, including frustration tolerance, flexibility, emotion regulation, and problem solving. All of these skills would have come into play in the short time she and the officer hashed out a suitable solution.

What's the practical and more effective alternative to punishments and rewards? My colleagues and I teach an approach called Collaborative Problem Solving (CPS), which Dr. Ross Greene originated in the book *The Explosive Child* and which we outlined together in the book *Treating Explosive Kids*.[1] CPS includes a philosophical component, or way of thinking, as well as a practical, problem-solving method we call Plan B.[2] The latter is a structured conversation such as the one I alluded to above, a process for solving problems. It brings two people together on equal ground, allowing each to articulate his or her perspective, and allowing them to collaborate on a solution. Instead of parents, teachers, police officers, and others imposing their authority, they engage more compassionately with the people under their care, helping them to practice and develop skills by inviting them to help generate solutions. If Plan B sounds unrealistic, you should know that conversations like this are occurring across the world in all kinds of settings with the world's most challenging people. I'll provide a number of examples and present data about the dramatic results achieved using CPS in the chapters that follow.

THREE STRATEGIES FOR HANDLING PROBLEMS WITH OTHERS

"Plan A" = Impose your will

"Plan B" = Solve the problem collaboratively

"Plan C" = Drop your expectation for now[3]

Plan B Isn't "Soft"

When they first learn about Plan B, parents, teachers, executives, police officers, and others schooled in conventional discipline routinely object that the approach is too soft. "You're just letting people do what they want," they'll say. They'll wag their fingers at me. "You can't do that. These people will walk all over you. They'll chew you up and spit you out!"

Plan B is not at all about relinquishing your expectations. In Plan B, you're aggressively pursuing your expectations and concerns, but you're doing it *without imposing your solution*. You've made a request: "Max, clean your room," or "Alicia, I need those evaluations by the end of the day." When a person doesn't comply, you're choosing to engage in *a structured and collaborative dialogue.* You're sticking by your concern and asking the noncompliant person to work with you to craft a solution that addresses what both of you care about.

Many people wrongly equate firmly asking someone to do something with conventional discipline. They assume that posing a firm request is inconsistent with Plan B. I once had one of our trainers from Ottawa, Canada, down to visit my family in Boston, and we invited her and her family to come to the pool with us. My daughter was racing around the pool, and I barked at her: "Paige, stop running!" Our trainer looked at me with a smile and said, "Wow, Mr. Plan A!" I shook my head. "Actually, that's not conventional discipline. That's asking her to stop running around the pool. Now, if she doesn't listen to me, then you will get to see whether I use Plan B." You can be firm with people in initially communicating your expectations. Sometimes you *need* to be firm. That's consistent with Plan B. What happens *after* you've articulated your expectations and they are not met is the decisive point. Do you attempt to impose your will, threatening a reward or punishment? Or do you air out your views and come together to collaborate on a solution?

In correctional facilities, staff will often ask me: "If I do Plan B, how will they learn to take responsibility for their actions?" I respond by noting that Plan B hardly absolves the challenging person of responsibility for their actions. On the contrary: You're *increasing* their level of responsibility. There is nothing easy about working with another person to generate a mutually satisfactory solution. Plan B is hard work, and the offender is on the hook to do that work. From this perspective, conventional rewards and punishments are the softer option. By dictating a solution, you're absolving the challenging person of helping to craft a solution. All the offender has to do with conventional discipline is passively receive a set of consequences. There's no more powerful way to hold someone accountable than to say, "You have to participate in a process to solve a problem that you've caused so that it doesn't happen again."

Applying Plan B

As I've suggested, Plan B yields long-term solutions for challenging behavior—it helps people build their underlying thinking skills in the process of solving problems collaboratively in the moment. Before examining how this is true, let's first take a closer look at Plan B and how we might best apply it. In this chapter's opening scenario, the safety officer embraced a Plan A response, attempting to impose his solution. That's what most individuals and institutions resort to in conflict situations. Plan A is a lesson in *might makes right*. It creates extrinsic motivation for good behavior but fails to instill *intrinsic* motivation—the drive to do well that arises when people feel independent, empowered, and passionate about what they're doing, and connected with others. When applied to people with skill struggles, Plan A also throws emotional fuel on the fire, often escalating challenging behavior.

If the school safety officer had decided to ignore the girl's disrespectful language and let her violate the rules, he might have been practicing Plan C. In Plan C, a person decides to withdraw a demand or expectation for the time being. Plan C is not the same as giving in. It is a strategic choice. A person choosing Plan

C prioritizes which problems to address, realizing that you can't deal with every problem all at once. By saving some problems or unmet expectations for later while addressing higher-priority problems now, we can reduce some challenging behaviors. In our real-life scenario, the security officer would remain in charge when using Plan C, because he is the one deciding what to address and what to drop for now. He might simply have decided this was not the best time to try to solve that problem, and that letting the student reenter the school was worth the risks.

The heart of Collaborative Problem Solving is Plan B, a conversation through which people in conflict work together to solve problems in mutually satisfactory and practical ways. Plan B is comprised of three basic steps:

- Step 1: Empathize—clarify their concerns.
- Step 2: Share your own concerns.
- Step 3: Invite the other person to brainstorm solutions with you, so that you can arrive at one that is both practical and mutually satisfactory.

In the second version of our scenario, the safety officer first empathizes with the girl by affirming that he understands her point of view. He gets what she's going through and why she's upset. But he hardly stops there. Once he has calmed her by empathizing and reassuring her that he doesn't want to impose his solution, he expresses what *he* cares about: "I'm not allowed to let people in. There are rules, and if I bend them for you, I could lose my job." With both sets of concerns clearly expressed, he goes on to work with the student to collaboratively investigate possible solutions. "What can we do to get you your bus pass *without* me breaking the rules? Any ideas?" After some discussion and collaboration, the two arrive at a solution, quite possibly one neither had originally considered.

The point of Collaborative Problem Solving is not to use Plan B exclusively in moments of conflict. Rather, it's to realize that when you have a problem with someone—when someone is not meeting an expectation of yours or is misbehaving in your eyes— you have three options from which to choose. You don't have to go straight to imposing your authority. At times, of course, you might want or need to impose your authority. In those cases, you choose Plan A. This approach allows you to attempt to impose your solution, but it doesn't reduce challenging behavior, build the underlying skills, or create or restore a helping relationship.

At other times, when you just want to maintain some calm, it might make sense to go with Plan C and proactively accept their solution. Plan C will reduce challenging behavior for now, but, again, you aren't building any underlying skills or helping to forge a strong helping relationship. Also, you aren't addressing your own concerns in the situation at hand.

If you want to arrive at durable solutions and help another person build the skills they need to meet your expectations in the future, Plan B is the only way to go. Also, if you want to build a helpful relationship with another person, then, again, go with Plan B.

You can use Plan B to de-escalate a crisis in the heat of the moment, as in the school safety example above. Dr. Greene first referred to that as "Emergency Plan B."[4] But the far more

GOALS ACHIEVED BY THE THREE PLANS

GOALS	PLAN A	PLAN C	PLAN B
Try to get your expectation met	✔	✘	✔
Reduce challenging behavior	✘	✔	✔
Build skills, confidence	✘	✘	✔
Solve problems	✘	✘	✔
Build relationships	✘	✘	✔

preferable approach is to deploy what he called "Proactive Plan B" *strategically* to prevent ongoing or predictable problems you have with someone.[5] In the latter case, you'll first want to think about which problems you want to pursue, and in what order. It helps to start modestly, addressing expectations of yours in areas that the other person cares about and where you're able to show more flexibility. Once you've put the process on a firm footing, you can proceed to more difficult problems (i.e., problems that happen more frequently and where you don't have much room to bend your expectations).

It's important to be realistic about when you can use Plan B and when you may need to revert back to attempting to impose authority (Plan A). When immediate safety is at issue and a situation risks getting out of hand, you might need to use Plan A. One juvenile detention guard we worked with, a naysayer who became a true believer in Plan B, had a saying: "If the kid's still talking, I'm still doing B." He meant that a kid could pick up a metal chair, hold it over his head, and look like he's about to smash it over your head, but if he was still talking, this guard would not radio for help and try to take him down. He would try to calm the child using words, reassuring him that he was not trying to impose his will.

I find that remarkable, but honestly, I don't know if I would do the same. Just because a kid or an adult is still talking doesn't mean I'm not concerned enough to go back to Plan A. In these situations, there's no shame in using Plan A, and sometimes a person will even thank you later for doing so. You'll need to save Plan B for another day, when cooler heads have returned.

Understand a Problem in Order to Solve It

Plan B seems simple—only three steps. But there are some important nuances. When you're using Plan B and starting a conversation with someone, follow the steps in their exact order. Albert Einstein once remarked that "the formulation of the problem is often more essential than its solution." That's true in science, and it's true when solving problems in everyday life. Don't rush to the third step—brainstorming a solution. Take time to formulate the problem by first completing the initial two steps well. Dr. Greene reminds us to define a problem "simply as two concerns that have yet to be reconciled."[6] So to formulate a problem well you need to spend time unpacking those two sets of concerns.

If you approach someone else to try to solve a problem, the other person will often assume that what you *really* want is to have him comply with your wishes. Such assumptions arise most frequently when a power differential exists in a relationship and you, as the more powerful person, are initiating the conversation. If you were to start right in by expressing your concern, you would seem to be confirming this assumption. The conversation would seem to the other person like Plan A. As a result, the person would likely become defensive or, as often is the case when a power differential exists, shut down. In professional language, we call the latter dissociative compliance: checking out and saying whatever you think the person holding the power wants to hear.

By first empathizing and clarifying the other person's concerns, you let him know that the conversation isn't like others he might have experienced—that you're working very hard to understand his concerns so as to solve the problem at hand. Just listening to a person and eliciting his thoughts has a calming effect, opening the way for further progress. Many people think that empathy is something you express to someone. In truth, *empathy* means "to understand." To gain that understanding, you must ask questions, reflect what you hear, take educated guesses, be patient, and try to peek behind someone's proposed solutions to glimpse their underlying concerns. Once you've clarified the other person's concerns, then, and only then, should you express your concerns. As this is a collaborative process, it's the *combination* of concerns that properly frames the problem or issue at hand. From there, you can both proceed to the third step, brainstorming a solution.

The order of steps in Plan B corresponds to what neuroscience

Empathy means "to understand."

has revealed about brain functioning. The brain processes information sequentially, from the bottom up. You need to address more primitive responses first before proceeding to engage the more rational parts of the brain. Otherwise, you'll fail. The empathy step first operates at the level of the brain stem, the most primal part of the brain, which helps people regulate their emotions. The midbrain, where the limbic system is located and which helps people relate to others, is engaged when an individual experiences another person's empathy. It's also engaged during the second step, when an individual is hearing the other person's perspective. The last step, collaborating to arrive at a solution, engages the prefrontal cortex, the rational part of the brain. The sequence goes like this: regulate, relate, reason. You can't ask the human brain to perform those steps out of order—you can't access the cortex without first going through the brain stem and the midbrain.[7] If you follow Plan B as I've outlined, you won't make that mistake.[8]

Think of Plan B as akin to the task of painting a room. You might feel impatient to jump to the end of the process and start putting paint on the wall. But if you don't slow down and put the prep work in, the finished product won't turn out well. It's not fun to move out the furniture, lay down the drop cloth, tape the edges, sand the walls, and so on, but this prep work makes the actual painting go smoothly later on. With Plan B, creating solutions to problems together with another person is the easy part if you first put in the hard work of the initial two ingredients. Most of your time, in fact, will be spent in Steps 1 and 2. We may want to rush to solutions, possibly because we want to help or are

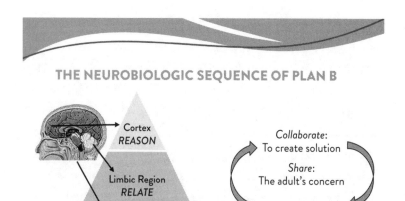

THE NEUROBIOLOGIC SEQUENCE OF PLAN B

Cortex
REASON

Limbic Region
RELATE

MidBrain/Brainstem
REGULATE

Collaborate:
To create solution

Share:
The adult's concern

Empathize:
Clarify the child's concern

Reflective listening
Reassurance

pressed for time. It's important to hold back on potential solutions until you have first expressed and understood each other's concerns.

Step 1: Empathize

Of the three steps, empathy can prove especially difficult. Most struggle with this complicated skill, or we may simply fail to apply our skill fully in the heat of the moment because our own cortex is closed for business. It's not so easy to empathize with a kid who shouts "fuck you" at you at the top of his lungs, or who has just gone on a rampage and kicked a hole in your wall. It's also hard to empathize with people who are reluctant to communicate their feelings because they fear Plan A, or who are unable to do so because of their skill struggles.

Your own status as an authority figure can also handicap you. In many contexts, authority figures are trained to speak or behave in ways that affirm their importance and power. Think of how judges sit on podiums, higher up than everyone else, wearing formal black robes. Or think of the stern, authoritarian tones that many police officers are trained to adopt. If you're trying to apply Plan A, the trappings of power help. If you're trying to encourage someone to express her concerns so that you can understand them, they're toxic. Power differentials are inherently dysregulating, and they are misleading. We think they will induce compliance. In truth, they induce what I described earlier as dissociative, or fake, compliance.

Over time, in the course of engaging in countless Plan B conversations and reviewing hundreds recorded by others in all kinds of settings, I've discovered that doing four things—and only four things—during the empathy step best enables us to learn about people's concerns so that we can empathize with them, even if we're in positions of power. First, ask lots of clarifying questions. Second, if your questions don't get you anywhere, hazard some guesses at what might be bothering the other person. Third, practice reflective listening (i.e., repeat back what the person says in your own words in order to clarify it—don't just spit it back verbatim). Fourth, reassure the other person that you're just trying to understand her point of view and not trying to impose your will.

The first two strategies help to elicit information. The second two calm the other person and make it easier to access information that might be hard to obtain if he is upset or suspicious of your motives. To perform the empathy step well, toggle back and forth between these four tools, taking care to listen closely. We call this active listening, which means listening to understand rather than to respond.

Let's say you're a teacher and your class is supposed to be doing silent, independent work. One girl is talking and disrupting other students. You might ask, "What's going on? Why aren't you doing your work?"

"Because it's stupid. I hate it," she might say.

You might feel tempted to cut the conversation short or explain why the work isn't stupid. The girl just doesn't want to talk, and further questioning would seem fruitless. Or, in an attempt to show empathy, you might say, "Well, you might think it's stupid. I can understand that. But here's why it's important." Does that sound like empathy? It isn't. In this case, you have stopped listening and are imposing your point of view, albeit gently. We call this "drive-by empathy." Rather than taking time to probe and hear someone out, you take a casual turn at empathy before quickly moving on and returning to the standard authority figure–subject relationship.

Don't shortchange the empathy step. Instead, use the four tools to slow down and unpack the other person's concerns. When the girl says, "I hate it," you can respond by taking her to the hallway, so that the other students aren't distracted from their work, and saying, "All right, I hear you. You say you hate it. What do you hate about it?" That's reflective listening, followed by a clarifying question. Stay with the girl, even if her attitude bothers you. Try to tease out her perspective. Just doing that signals that you take her seriously and that you care. It calms her, and once she's calm, the more rational parts of her brain can engage.

Suppose she's still intransigent or belligerent. She might say, "I'm not talking to you. I can do what I want." What do you do then? She's shutting down with this comment, so we're going to have to go back to one of our calming tools: *reassurance*. "You know," you might say, "you're not in trouble. That's not what this is about. I bet there's a good reason why you're not sitting down and doing your work. I just want to understand what that reason is." Such reassurance again helps to regulate the person's emotions at the level of the brain stem, and it may be especially necessary if you haven't practiced Plan B with this girl before (it takes time to build trust and rapport). When the girl seems calmer, you might pose a question again, maybe even taking an educated guess: "I notice that sometimes you get your independent work done pretty quickly, and then you're stuck sitting there waiting for everyone else to finish. Do you suppose that maybe when you're finished you have a hard time sitting still, and so instead of starting it in the first place, you just decide not to do it?"

The empathy step is really just about being a good detective. It's about probing, investigating, all the while calming and reassuring the other person. And it's about starting the conversation in a neutral way that will engage the other person, so that you can obtain useful information. Of course, the worst time to solve a predictable problem is right when it is happening yet again. You'll have more luck obtaining information when the moment of conflict has passed.

I once had a chance to train all the juvenile and family court judges in New York City. As I taught them Plan B, emphasizing the need to find a neutral way of starting the conversation, one of the tough, skeptical judges interrupted. "Wait a minute. Let me get this straight. You want me from the bench in my courtroom to say something like, 'Hey, I've noticed that the last time you were here, I gave you a choice between jail and community service, and it seems like you picked community service, and yet you didn't show up. What's up with that?'" All the other judges laughed.

"Actually," I said, "that's exactly what I want you to ask, although if you can do it without the sarcasm, you might actually get some useful information." I was, I admit, a little cranky.

As I went on to explain, it was worth trying to get the defendant in this situation to open up, because the information he might yield would prove critical. The defendant had a choice between jail and community service, and he initially picked the latter, as would anyone in his right mind. However, because the defendant didn't show up for his service, he is headed to jail. If we don't come to understand why, we'll never help the defendant solve the problem in a better way. The defendant's choice not to show up was exceedingly poor, but there were probably important concerns (like transportation issues) and skill struggles (such as poor planning) that led to it. If we can address those concerns and build skills without compromising our own expectations, we'll arrive at solutions that are better for everyone.

The same holds true for the challenging behavior you're seeing from your kids, partner, colleagues, bosses—anyone. Yes, the behavior is unacceptable, but the person who is misbehaving likely has important concerns and skill struggles that cause her to act the way she does. We are all doing the best we can with the skills we have. If she isn't doing well, we need to slow down, investigate, and identify the underlying concerns. Be curious, and prepare yourself for surprises.

FOUR USEFUL EMPATHY TOOLS

1. Ask clarifying questions.
2. Take guesses about what might be bothering the other person.
3. Practice reflective listening.
4. Reassure the other person that you're not trying to impose your will.

Step 2: Share Your Concerns

At the end of the first step of Plan B, the empathy step, the other person in the conversation should feel calmer and understood. Then, and only then, can you share *your own* concerns. If you're having a Plan B conversation proactively about a recurring problem, you might take time before the conversation to think and clarify your concerns and even to plan what you're going to say. If you're applying Plan B on the fly or in a crisis situation, make sure you articulate your concerns and don't just rush into announcing your proposed solution. Tell the other person what worries you. Maybe you're concerned about the person's health, safety, learning, or emotional well-being. Maybe it's the impact of that person's behavior on someone else. Whatever the case, clue in the other person. Give him the opportunity to understand your perspective. And be as specific as possible.

The wording you use matters. Don't follow up the empathy step by saying, "I hear you, but . . ." This only reinforces the notion that the concern you're about to state is more important than the other person's. For Plan B to work, your perspectives have to take on equal standing. Say instead, "I understand what you're saying. You are saying [repeat what the other person has said]. Here's what I'm worried about. Here is what is on my mind." It's not "I hear you, but . . ." Rather, it's "I hear you *and . . .*"

If stating your perspective causes the other person to become more emotional or, conversely, to shut down, don't worry. This is normal, and it stems from the other person's fear that your statement of your concern has just diminished the importance of her concern. Go back to the empathy step and reassure the other person that you haven't forgotten her concern. Reregulate her before moving up the brain again. If it seems like the other person doesn't share your concern, again, don't worry—she doesn't have to. She just has to take your concern into consideration.

Step 3: Brainstorm Solutions

When you've expressed your perspective and the other person is still reasonably calm, you've completed the second step. At this point, you have two sets of concerns. Not two sets of solutions— two sets of *concerns*, two points of view. Now you can move to the third and final step: working together to generate a mutually satisfactory solution. It is helpful to start the brainstorming by recapping both sets of concerns so that it's clear what you're trying to do. Then bite your tongue and ask the other person in the conversation to generate the first solution or set of solutions. You might say, "I bet there is something we can think of so that your concern and mine are both addressed." The police officer in the scenario above might prompt the student by saying, "I'll bet there's a way that you can get your bus pass so you can get to where you want to go, and, at the same time, I don't have to break any rules. Do you have any ideas?" Giving the other person the first chance to brainstorm is crucial, because it helps her have a sense of ownership over both the process and the eventual solution. Also, it gives her a chance to build her problem-solving skills.

It may be that the other person doesn't offer any ideas. In that case, you can reassure her, saying, "It's all right. Don't worry. If you don't have any ideas, I bet we can come up with some. Let me think for a second and see if I have an idea." But suppose the person does offer an idea, and it's a bad one. What then? Regardless of the quality of the other person's idea, take it seriously. Respond by saying something like "That's one idea. Let's think about it together." Then perform an analysis of it together, evaluating whether it works for each party, and also whether it's realistic and feasible. If you went with the proposed solution, would you create new problems?

If the girl seeking the bus pass says, "Let me go in there and get my stupid bus pass! This whole thing is stupid," you can say, "That's one idea, you getting the pass. Let's think about that. If you get the pass, that works for you. Then I'm letting you back in, and whether you think that's a stupid rule or not, you've broken the rule. It's my job to obey the rules, so that doesn't work so well for me. Stick with me, I think we can figure this out so that it works for both of us. There must be something we can come up with that lets you get your bus pass and we aren't breaking any rules. Any ideas?" By taking time to spell out the logic, you're modeling the use of all kinds of skills, such as empathizing, perspective taking, flexible thinking, impulse control, and emotion regulation.

Proceeding like this, you and the other person can suggest constructive solutions and analyze them together. In the case of the girl seeking the bus pass, either the police officer or the girl might suggest ideas like "I wonder if we can get a friend of yours to go get it," or "I wonder if one of the other officers could go get it," or "I wonder if we can have an officer accompany you." The point is to arrive at a workable solution that addresses both concerns. More than that, it's to engage in a *process* of collaborative problem solving. The process is how the underlying skills get built—executive functioning skills such as generating multiple solutions to a problem and forecasting (testing out ideas before acting upon them), communication skills, emotion regulation skills, and the list goes on. The process itself is where the magic is.

> The process itself is where the magic is.

Throughout the brainstorming step, stay positive and evoke your belief that together you *will* come up with a great solution acceptable to both parties. Affirm that you're as invested in ensuring that the other person's concerns get addressed as you are in seeing your own concerns addressed. Also, work with whatever ideas the other person puts forward. Look for ways to combine, expand, modify, and build on ideas. When you've arrived at a mutually satisfactory and practical solution, as well as a follow-up plan for enacting it, then you're done—you've completed Plan B.

Skill Building with Plan B

You might wonder: Does CPS *really* build underlying problem-solving skills? In fact, it does. Our research team at Massachusetts General Hospital and our collaborators have amassed empirical, quantitative evidence showing that CPS helps kids build underlying skills. In one study, we assessed the skills development of hundreds of kids who received CPS as part of their day treatment at Crossroads Children's Center in Ottawa, Canada. We compared these kids to thousands of other kids in the Canadian province of Ontario who received similar services but not CPS. The kids who had engaged in CPS with adults showed greater improvements in their symptoms and functioning. Further analysis showed that improvement in underlying self-regulation (impulse control) and cognitive flexibility skills were associated with these clinical improvements.[9] In addition, we found that CPS changed the way adults thought about the kids, which affected how they interacted with them. This, too, helped account for the clinical improvements the kids experienced.

It may seem strange to think that having a Plan B conversation is better for skill building than performing tasks in a therapist's office, in a skills group, or on a smartphone app. Yet it absolutely is. Removing people from everyday life to train them in skills they have to use *in* everyday life doesn't work. A prime example is anger management classes. These classes convene people with emotional regulation issues, teaching them what they should do when they are angry—as if they don't already know these things. The challenge isn't *knowing* what to do. It's accessing the rational part of the brain in the heat of the moment so that you can *apply* what you know. The way to overcome anger management problems is to help a person practice controlling his emotions in the moment. It's hanging in there with that person, tamping down his emotional response enough so that he can start to think rationally. And it's doing that repetitively, day after day, so that new pathways in the brain can form.

Neuroscientists explain the way skills get built by referring to the specificity principle of neuroplasticity. To change a neural network, you have to activate *that actual neural network*.[10] But artificial circumstances don't recruit the actual neural networks involved in applying specific skills. You need real life for that. Plan B allows people to practice skills in the very environments in which they will need to apply them. And, critically, it does so in those small and necessary doses of what neurobiologists call good stress. You can't change a person's stress response without activating their stress response. The dilemma is how to stress the brain safely, without causing new trauma. Healthy stress is moderate, predictable, and controlled—exactly what Plan B affords. Applying Plan B repetitively over the course of the day to address specific conflict situations, authority figures or caregivers can deliver small doses of stress, gradually carving new pathways in people's brains.

Plan B conveys other skill-building benefits as well. When engaged in a Plan B conversation, people don't build just one skill at a time. As we saw in the above scenario, they build many skills at once. It is rare that we need to deploy a single skill in isolation. Rather, we have to apply a bunch of skills together simultaneously in real life. Further, Plan B automatically builds precisely the skills that need the most work. If a person possesses strong language and communication skills, she'll have no problem articulating her own concerns. That part of the Plan B conversation will proceed smoothly. When you get to the second part of the conversation and it's time for this person to listen to and appreciate your concerns, she might have more trouble, perhaps because perspective taking and empathizing isn't her strength. The conversation will naturally get bogged down here, leading both of you to slow down and work harder to practice this skill. Plan B, in other words, provides a natural and indirect assessment of a person's skills. Instead of the usual one-size-fits-all training, working through problems collaboratively offers an approach tailored to the specific needs of each participant.

When I present Plan B to people, they often wonder what happens if the authority figures (parents, teachers, managers, therapists, police officers, and so on) engaging in the Plan B conversation lack skills themselves. Does that mess everything up? The bad news is that many of us authority figures do indeed have our own skill struggles. The good news is that authority figures also practice their skills during Plan B. If you tend to get angry quickly, your emotional regulation skills might need some work. Or perhaps you're less adept at social thinking than you think—you're not understanding how you are coming across or impacting others as well as you might. Plan B is collaborative in the deepest sense.

Not only are the participants collaborating on coming up with solutions to specific problems; they're also collaborating to improve the thinking skills they need to resolve conflicts.

The latest research is turning up empirical evidence that parents using Plan B with their kids develop empathy skills over time. Researchers followed forty-two families of small children (age three to twelve) who had undergone a twelve-week CPS program in their homes. Each week, a caseworker trained in CPS went to each family's home two to three times, observing interactions between family members, teaching Plan B, and offering advice about how to apply the approach. Before and after the treatment window, caseworkers assessed how well the children behaved, how well the children used executive functioning skills, and how stressed parents were. Parents also filled out questionnaires before and after treatment that allowed researchers to assess their empathy levels as well as other variables related to CPS. Results suggested that behavioral difficulties among children declined significantly, in part because children developed better executive functioning skills. But there was also a significant improvement in how competent *parents* were at understanding other people's perspectives. Plan B had built their skills, not merely their children's.[11]

Plan B affords still another benefit: It teaches skills in a *relational* context. You can't change a relational pattern unless you are engaged in a relational interaction. In

> People tend to learn better in the context of relationships.

addition, as neuroscience teaches us, people tend to learn better in the context of relationships. In fact, all healthy human development occurs in the relational context of interactions with others. Remove that context (through parental neglect, for instance) and you arrest brain development. To take a less severe example, if you ask school-age kids which classes they like, you usually find that the answer has more to do with the teacher and his teaching style than with the class's actual content. Really good teachers forge relationships with students while engaging with them in hands-on activities, and those relationships help the content establish itself in the brain. With Plan B, people are practicing skills experientially via a conversation that serves as a vehicle for relationship building. Plan A, as we've seen, causes relationships to break down. As people solve problems together via Plan B, they build trust and understanding. The skills become even more quickly and firmly embedded.

If you want to learn how to play a Bach invention on the piano, the way to learn the complex skills required isn't to sit in a classroom and have someone lecture to you. Nor is it to do exercises that simulate a Bach invention. The way to learn is to actually try to play the piece in the presence of a piano teacher. You stumble over weak areas, and the teacher gives you the feedback you need in the moment. You practice again and again, receiving more correction. Over time, you develop a relationship with the teacher. New pathways form in your brain. You develop the skills you need. And you get better at playing the piece.

"Tell me and I forget," Ben Franklin once said, "teach me and I may remember, involve me and I learn." Such involvement is precisely what conventional discipline precludes, and what Plan B provides. This is not to say that Plan B builds skills or repairs relationships instantaneously. It takes time and practice. Some skills develop more easily than others, depending on how complex the skill is and how much of a deficit existed in the first place. When we work with people who have a hard time articulating their concerns, we can teach them basic language skills over the course of a few weeks of repetitive practice. Afterward, a person who used to act out will be able to say something like "I need a break," or "I can't talk about that right now." A much more difficult skill to build is empathy—the ability to consider someone else's perspective. That takes months, sometimes years, of hard work, with lots and lots of repetition. But if you put in the work, you will see results.

As I've seen in my clinical practice, we can even build skills among patients who struggle so much that they can't engage productively in Plan B conversations in the beginning. I've worked with countless patients on the autism spectrum, for instance, who struggle with extreme inflexibility. When you conduct the brainstorming step of Plan B with them, they fail to generate any ideas for solving the problem at hand, no matter how or how often you ask them. In these cases, we scaffold the process to help build the skill. Almost always, we see progress eventually.

Sometimes, for instance, we help inflexible patients build skills by giving them an easy framework they can use to solve problems. We tell them that there are three basic approaches to solving problems—compromising, asking for help, and trying something in a different way.[12] We help them to deploy this framework in real-life situations as they arise to spur creative thinking about more specific solutions.

A girl I worked with who is on the autism spectrum—I'll call her Shawna—represented these three approaches as images. When we needed to solve a problem together and had no ideas, she used these images as a visual prompt. She represented asking for help as a pail because that approach worked in so many situations—it was a big container into which she could throw many problems. Compromise was an Easter egg basket because "when people compromise, everybody ends up happy. That's nice. That's why there's nice flowery things in it." She represented trying something in a different way as a trash can because she "hated that one." Because she had trouble with flexible thinking, this option was especially difficult for her.

In therapy sessions, I'd walk Shawna through these three options as we tried to solve problems together using Plan B. When she couldn't come up with ideas, I'd point to the picture and say, "Let's walk through these options. Could we ask for help? If we did, whom would we ask? How would we go about doing that?" Then we'd explore the compromise option. "What would a compromise look like? Would it work?" If a compromise didn't seem feasible, we'd explore how she might go about solving the problem in a different way. We practiced this framework together so much that she came to internalize it, using it on her own to solve problems in her life. Plan B conversations with her have become easier, allowing for even more skill building going forward.

Other techniques exist to help remediate other varieties of

inflexible thinking in individuals with severe deficiencies. When performing Plan B with someone who possesses a deeply entrenched, black-and-white view of the world, I often teach flexibility by purposely challenging, or "graying up," her conceptual categories. I'll do it by borrowing a technique from Aaron Beck, the father of cognitive therapy, and challenging her to look at the data objectively together.

Let's say a child tells me that she hates everyone at school. "You hate everyone?" I'll respond.

"Yes, I do."

"Wow, so you hate everyone. What do you mean by 'hate'?"

"They're stupid and they're useless. They're *so* annoying."

"Well," I'll suggest, "I wonder whether maybe it's possible that even one person might *occasionally* sometimes be somewhat tolerable. I don't know. What do you think?"

After I gently push an inflexible child in this way, I ask her to think about how we could determine where the truth lies, remaining open-minded to the possibility that her version of the truth might be substantiated. In most cases, however, she will eventually concede that, yes, there is at least one person who might be somewhat tolerable, or even more than one. Little by little, through conversations like this, even extremely inflexible thinkers become a bit more flexible. They learn to see the world in shades of gray rather than in black and white. Plan B conversations become easier, leading to even more skill building in the future.

For anybody struggling with challenging behavior, one of the best things about Plan B as a form of skills training is that you don't have to point out that the person lacks a skill in order to help him develop it. The person doesn't have to agree or admit that he's weak in a certain area, nor does he have to be willing to work on it. All he has to be willing to do is solve a problem collaboratively in a way that works out for him, too. The skills training is smuggled in through the back door—for all parties involved.

Remember the Good Inside

Back in the early 2000s, when we were still in the early stages of developing CPS, I treated a young man I'll call Brendon. A smart guy from a middle-class, highly educated family, Brendon suffered from a rare skin disease that caused him to bruise easily. If he tripped and fell, he would bruise and start to bleed, requiring skin grafts and other treatments. All of this was hard on him, damaging his self-esteem. He started hanging out with the wrong crowd at school, smoking pot, and slacking on his homework. His parents responded with Plan A, removing all of his privileges, grounding him, and threatening to send him to a wilderness program, by force if need be.

I worked hard to help his parents try to maintain an empathic stance and believe that Brendon was doing the best he could and lacked skill, not will. During our sessions, I taught Brendon and his family how to do Plan B. Meanwhile, I lobbied his parents to back away from Plan A and give Plan B a chance to work. I feared that forcing Brendon into a therapeutic wilderness program to scare him straight would traumatize him, without benefiting him very much. Brendon also assured me that he wasn't smoking marijuana anymore. He claimed that his parents didn't understand him and were wrongly accusing him.

At one point in the midst of all this tension and drama, I brought Brendon into my office for a private conversation. I told him that I believed in him. "If you're telling me the truth," I said, "I want to help you. I want to advocate for you."

"I promise, man," he said. "I'm telling you the truth. I'm not smoking anymore." At this very moment, he shifted around in his chair, and what should fall out of his pocket but a big bag of marijuana. I couldn't believe it. And, I will admit, I was *pissed*. Brendon had been lying to my face for weeks. I had been trying to help him, taking his side, and all along he had been disrespecting me.

Not long afterward, his mother came into my office by herself, utterly bereft and not knowing what to do about her son. "I don't want to send him away," she said, weeping, "but I have no other options. When I look back at what a sweet kid he used to be, I can't believe he turned out so bad." She showed me a picture she found of her son when he was just three or four. It was a grainy photograph of him lying across the backseat of a car, sound asleep. He looked angelic there, the sweetest little kid. "See," she said, "he didn't used to be such an awful kid. He's just different now. He's not the same person. There's no sweetness there anymore. And it's our fault. We're good people, with good values, but we must have done something wrong."

I took a long look at the picture and became overwhelmed with emotion. My own kids were small at the time, my oldest boy about the same age as her son was in the picture. Brendon had once been like my son—full of hope, full of possibility, loving, caring, sweet, adorable. How awful and tragic that he no longer was like this. I told myself that we just had to find the good in Brendon. Because inside that tough, scary young man, there still was this wonderful little kid. I knew it. And so I kept working with Brendon, reenergized to help. We figured out that Brendon had a lot of difficulty managing anxiety and disappointment and predicting the consequences of his actions, and we worked on building those skills.

I think of this moment often when I'm teaching Plan B and working with challenging kids. It's hard engaging with people whose behavior upsets, frustrates, or even repulses us. It's hard to draw close to them, to hear them out, and to partner with them in solving a problem when really what we want to do is punish them. Often, they are telling us that they don't want to partner with us—in fact, they are screaming this at us, with a few expletives thrown in. Still, if we can remember the innocent child inside, engaging with them becomes a little easier. On so many occasions when I've become frustrated with Plan B, I think of Brendon and that picture. I remember the guiding philosophy of *skill, not will*, and I feel inspired to stay strong and keep working at it.

I can't say for sure whether Plan B made a difference for Brendon. I do know that he graduated from high school, went on to college, and did well. Although life was not always smooth for him, he managed to pull himself together. Plan B must have played a role, because for many years, long after I had stopped seeing Brendon, his mother dropped by my office around Thanksgiving and presented me with a chocolate pecan pie she had baked. I hadn't given her a magic bullet with CPS, but I had given her a viable alternative to the conventional way we try to handle challenging behavior. I had shown her how to build up her son's skills and her own at the same time, not by punishing him or sending him away, but by drawing closer and inviting him in on an equal footing to solve problems. I showed her something to do other than Plan A, which hadn't solved the problems and threatened to ruin their relationship as well. I had given her an approach that really does get meaningful results—one situation, one skill, one kid at a time. In the next chapter we'll examine those results, exploring what happens when parents of even the toughest kids apply CPS in their homes.

CHAPTER FIVE

Parenting 2.0

It was week two of summer vacation, and Vicki felt guilty—she was already looking forward to the end of the month, when her ten-year-old daughter, Becca, would go off to camp. Becca wasn't having such a great time, either. For the past several days, she had moped around the house complaining that she was bored and had run out of things to do. She didn't have many friends around, and she'd already blown through several books from the library.

On this day, Becca had made her way onto the computer, even though her parents had revoked this privilege as punishment for a spat of misbehavior. As Becca reasoned, her punishment wasn't much of a problem. Her parents had said she was forbidden from *playing* games on the computer—her typical online pastime. Today she had something different in mind. Having tired of an online game in which kids could create and care for virtual pets, she'd found a site for more advanced (and presumably much older) users that practically seemed to require users to be computer programmers. This wasn't *play*, Becca thought. This was something serious. She was *designing* a game.

When Vicki came upstairs after doing the laundry, this subtlety was lost on her. She barked at Becca and sent her to her room for not complying with the punishment. "But this isn't a game!" Becca said, shrieking. "I'm *creating* something!"

"Save the lawyer routine, Becca," Vicki said, beyond frustrated with her daughter's attempts to litigate her way around every rule she set.

Becca stomped to her room and threw herself on her bed. "You're the meanest person ever. How am I going to finish the game I'm designing?"

After an hour of seething, Becca left her room, went to the den, and idly flipped on the TV. Her mom hadn't said anything about television. She accidentally hit a menu button and, continuing down this path she'd stumbled on, came to a screen called "Parental Controls." *That's exactly what I need*, she thought. *How would they like to be the ones controlled all the time?* She followed the prompts until she was asked to enter a code to block access to the TV. She went ahead and entered one. Now her parents would need *her* permission to do something for a change.

Later that night, Vicki discovered that the TV was locked. "Becca!" she wailed. "What have you done this time? Did you do something to lock the TV?"

After ten minutes of fighting, Vicki finally got her daughter to unlock the TV. "God, help me," she said to herself. "I wonder how some parents manage to enjoy their kids during the summer."

Challenging behavior is a tremendous issue for parents and

kids—it's the number-one reason pediatricians refer children for mental health services. Fortunately, CPS has proven effective at reducing challenging behavior. As many parents tell us, it's the *only* thing that works after traditional approaches have failed. Yet CPS isn't just for challenging kids. The mentality of *skill, not will* helps all parents understand their kids in a new way, easing conflict and paving the way for stronger relationships. As parents apply CPS to everyday situations, they avoid the one-size-fits-all thinking of most parenting wisdom, engaging with their children in customized ways to build skills. If their kids have good enough skills to be compliant when needed, they help them build more sophisticated problem-solving skills such as empathy, perspective taking, flexibility, and creativity, preparing them for success as adults. The process also ignites deeper forms of motivation, so that their kids feel driven to find and follow their own passions. Ultimately, CPS can help us raise a generation of kids who disavow the *might makes right* perspective embedded in traditional parenting models, and who instead try to resolve disputes more compassionately and collaboratively with others.

A Proven Method

As I related at the beginning of this book, CPS was first developed as an intervention that parents could use by themselves outside of therapy. The parents to whom we first taught it were very enthusiastic about CPS and how it was working with their challenging kids. Wishing to verify these results, we conducted and helped to facilitate several published scientific studies testing the efficacy of CPS in homes. The results were incredible. In one study published in the *Journal of Consulting and Clinical Psychology*,[1] our team convened a group of fifty elementary school-age children diagnosed with oppositional defiant disorder, a set of symptoms involving willful disobedience of authority. These kids also all had signs of depression or bipolar disorder as well.

We randomly assigned each child and his or her family to one of two types of treatment. One type of treatment was a standard ten-week course of behavior management therapy. As part of this therapy, the families learned about conventional explanations of defiance, and they also learned about traditional discipline, including how to use time-outs as well as stickers, tokens, and so on to track a child's behavior and determine rewards and punishments. The other type of treatment was training in CPS for an average of eleven weeks. Families learned about the concept of *skill, not will* and about the three basic plans for handling problems, and they also had a chance to practice applying Plan B in conflict situations.

My colleagues and I were the therapists providing the CPS treatment, and independent overseers also reviewed recordings of the sessions to verify that we were offering the proper treatment. As part of the experiment, we administered a series of standard tests to parents before and after the therapies to measure how positive their interactions with their children were and how much stress parents felt. We also had therapists and parents complete a standard survey that rated how much they felt the child's behavior had changed since the family had begun therapy sessions. The therapists completed the survey upon completion of treatment, the parents four months later.

The kids of parents trained in CPS exhibited significantly

more improvement in their behavior, as rated by both parents and the consulting therapists. Four months after treatment, 80 percent of the children whose families had been trained in CPS saw excellent improvements in behavior, as opposed to only 44 percent whose families had received the standard training. Other published studies of CPS have reported similar results. Researchers in Sweden delivered between six and ten sessions of CPS training to parents of seventeen Swedish elementary school students with oppositional defiant disorder. Both after this intervention and six months later, all children in the group saw reductions in behaviors associated with the disorder. Children also exhibited fewer behaviors associated with attention deficit hyperactivity disorder.[2] When taught to parents in group settings, CPS has proven equally effective.[3]

Over the years, we've documented similar results in a number of other settings where authority figures deal with kids, and, to some extent, act as surrogate parents. In schools, we've helped dramatically reduce the use of traditional disciplinary measures like detentions, suspensions, and expulsions. We've also seen dramatic improvements in the environment for staff—reductions in stress and in injuries sustained on the job. For instance, my colleagues and I taught the basics of CPS to all fifty-three hundred NYPD school safety agents, performing this work during the last week before the new school year started. At the time, CPS was one of a number of initiatives and regulatory changes embraced by the New York City schools. During the next school year, the number of arrests made in schools decreased by 58 percent over the previous year, the number of summonses issued by 67 percent, reports of major crimes by 20 percent, and reports of violent crimes by 39 percent.[4]

We have seen similar results in a number of schools across the country. At one Colorado school, a pilot study found that the stress on teachers fell significantly after they received training in CPS, and that the most significant reductions were for those teachers whose fidelity to the approach was highest. A number of schools designed for challenging kids saw reductions in the need for restraints, a reduction in suspensions and seclusions, and, in some cases, a near elimination of the need for these kinds of disciplinary practices. A school in New York State not only experienced a dramatic decline in the number of suspensions; there was a 48 percent increase in school attendance. Still other schools have reported greater confidence on the part of teachers in their general ability to work with students as well as improved relationships with students.[5]

In psychiatric facilities and juvenile prisons we've used CPS to dramatically reduce self-injurious behaviors and to reduce or *eliminate* the use of physical restraints or seclusion rooms to control behavior. After implementing CPS at Yale's child inpatient psychiatric unit, seclusions were reduced from 432 to 133 a year, and restraints were reduced from 263 to 7 a year.[6] In the year after it implemented CPS, the Ohio Hospital for Psychiatry cut its use of restraints by 95 percent and eliminated use of its seclusion room. Staff turnover, usually very high at psychiatric facilities, declined to under 3 percent per year. In Nova Scotia, Canada, one twelve-bed juvenile residential treatment program saw a 69 percent drop in seclusions during the six-month period after implementing CPS, and a 78 percent drop after forty months.[7] In a five-year study of one New York State hospital's adolescent inpatient psychiatric unit, researchers found that violent incidences (i.e., those requiring the use of restraints, those where patients harmed themselves, and those where staff had to call in security) fell from 182 in 2008 (prior to the implementation of CPS) to 86 in 2012.[8]

In recent years, entire systems of care have embraced CPS. The state of Oregon began introducing CPS through its Addictions and Mental Health division. Now virtually every agency in the state serving challenging kids uses some form of our approach, and more than fifty programs have implemented it comprehensively, including the juvenile correctional system and just about every therapeutic inpatient and residential program. As further evidence of the sustainability of systemic changes across Oregon, an administrative statute in the state now requires that all child-focused mental health agencies utilize approaches that involve "a collaborative process to solving problems with youth."

Finally, CPS has proven successful at juvenile detention facilities housing some of the toughest kids imaginable. A number of juvenile justice facilities in North America have implemented CPS. In one unpublished report from the Mountain View Youth Development Center in Maine, rates of assault and the use of force decreased by more than 50 percent, and time spent in seclusion decreased by more than 89 percent after staff had received training in CPS. Recidivism fell precipitously. In 2003, 60 percent of inmates had reoffended within one year of being released from the facility, whereas in 2008, after CPS had been introduced, only 15 percent of inmates reoffended. Fewer staff submitted claims for compensation due to injury as well.[9]

Overcoming the Myth of Consistency

CPS works well for parents and other authority figures dealing with challenging kids for a number of reasons. First, CPS affords parents a customized approach to handling their children's behavior problems. Most parents think that they have to parent each of their kids in the same way (if they have more than one), or that they should apply the same discipline to their child that their friends, neighbors, or family members might apply to theirs. They think that siblings will exploit any inconsistency in discipline, taking advantage or becoming resentful if both parents don't treat each kid exactly the same—that the individualized approach will be seen as unfair. Furthermore, moms and dads often come to me claiming that they and their spouse need to be aligned so that together they can parent consistently.

This myth of consistency, as I call it, is fruitless. If you parent each child in the same way, you ensure that *no child*

> If you parent each child in the same way, you ensure that *no child* gets what he or she needs.

gets what he or she needs. Research shows that children exhibit significant differences in personality and temperament, even if they share the same genes and grow up in the same basic environment.[10] As we've seen, the cognitive skills of children vary, reflecting underlying differences in their brain development. Some children might struggle with flexibility skills, while others are weak in communication skills, still others in social skills, and still others in multiple skill areas. Parenting decisions and tactics that might work for one child might not work well for another, even if the other one happens to be a sibling.

For parents raising multiple children, the goal shouldn't be consistency or fairness. It should be *matching your strategies and decisions to the needs of each individual child.* CPS prompts parents to identify each child's specific strengths and weaknesses from among the five basic skill areas we identified in chapter 2, and to note areas in which a child struggles. Due to deficits in the underlying skills, a more challenging child might struggle with a number of common, everyday situations, whereas her sibling doesn't. When a difficult situation arises, a parent might decide to handle the conflict by taking the time to problem solve with the child exhibiting challenging behavior and build skills. In that case, the parent would engage in Plan B with the child. With a sibling, the parent might go with Plan A despite its downsides, because the child already has the skills required to meet the parent's expectations. In other conflict situations involving the challenging kid, the parent might decide that skill building isn't a priority. In that case, the parent would strategically choose Plan A (asserting authority in the moment) or Plan C (handling the situation the way their kid wants for now). A parent who is in a hurry to make soccer practice might use Plan A in the moment to get her child to turn off the

TV and get ready to leave. If that parent is asked by the same child for permission to eat leftover Valentine's Day chocolates a half hour before dinner, she might agree to it, employing Plan C. Whatever course of action parents choose, they can make a decision for *each child* based on his or her *own unique needs.*

As we've seen, Plan B discussions address the uniqueness of individual children by naturally homing in on the specific areas of weakness that a child exhibits. If a child struggles with regulating emotions, that second step of Plan B—in which the parent expresses his concern—might pose the greatest difficulty. The parent would naturally need to return to the first step to calm the child with empathy and reassurance, building the underlying emotional regulation skills. As that skill improves, other parts of the Plan B conversation might become sticking points, leading the parent to work on different skills. In this way, Plan B conversations give kids practice with the specific skills that require the most work at any given point in time. In our clinical work, we find that Plan B conversations vary widely among children, even though the focus of the conflict at issue—not doing homework, for instance, or refusing to go to bed on time—might be identical.

More Compassion for Challenging Kids— and Their Parents

Beyond the usefulness of the CPS process, the mind-set shift underlying this approach affords a number of benefits to parents who confront challenging behavior. In many cases, so-called difficult kids happen to be extremely gifted in other ways. Like

Becca, the precocious and cognitively inflexible girl we met at the beginning of the chapter, they may be sensitive kids with impressive strengths in things like art, music, literature, math, or sports. They may have a strong sense of right and wrong and be easily moved by injustice. They may be animal lovers, chefs, debate masters, or theater buffs. Maybe the word *gifted* gets invoked. Maybe *artistic* or *quirky*. Or, simply, *intense*.

Despite their strengths, their challenging behavior still poses a problem. These kids may lose it around minor matters. Life may not go according to their plan, or they might fail to meet their own perfectionistic standards of achievement at school or elsewhere. They may resist trying anything at which they can't quickly excel because their world is so "all or nothing." Some may have trouble finding and keeping friends. In many cases, they may simply seem to *feel* too intensely, and struggle to manage their emotions effectively.

Parents dealing with challenging kids often find their noncompliant behavior puzzling. How can this kid be good at so many things, these adults wonder, and yet have so much trouble?

> Areas of great strength in kids can and often coexist with relative weaknesses.

The theory of *skill, not will* offers a compelling answer. When it comes to skills development, areas of great strength in kids can and often coexist with relative weaknesses, and these cognitive disparities can fuel behavior problems. We tend to think of kids by categorizing them as "smart," "talented," or "athletic," even though uneven, or asynchronous, cognitive development is the norm. When some areas of ability and brain development are indeed off the charts, even average or above-average functioning in other domains can amount to significant differences, or unevennesses, that make the world difficult for these kids to negotiate. Also, for most of us our greatest strength is also our greatest weakness. We might applaud kids for their perseverance, while frowning on their perseveration. Parents who understand the subtleties of cognitive development as well as how to address them gain a new sense of calm, comfort, and reassurance and a more precise way of helping their kids to succeed.

The notion of *skill, not will* also helps parents of challenging kids by alleviating the crushing guilt that many of them feel. When people encounter children who misbehave, and when they assume that children are doing it on purpose, they often blame the parents for not providing enough discipline. Kids act out, we think, because they're spoiled, or because they think they can get away with it due to lax parenting. Parents of challenging kids internalize this thinking, blaming themselves for being too passive, permissive, or inconsistent.

In truth, these explanations are inaccurate and unfair. Challenging kids are hard to raise—that's just a reality. Parents of such kids might appear more passive and permissive, but that doesn't cause bad behavior. That same parent would seem quite competent if he or she were raising an easier kid. I can't tell you how many parents I see in my clinic who have multiple children, one of whom is really challenging while the others are quite well behaved. The challenging behavior of the tough kids makes the parent appear clueless, even though he or she is not.

The solution isn't to cast judgment on parents, kids, or anyone else. Psychology and psychiatry have done much harm by blaming parents for problems we later learn weren't their fault. Believe it or not, as late as the 1980s we had a term for cold mothers whom we blamed for autism. We called them "refrigerator mothers." Likewise, during the early twentieth century, we blamed schizophrenia on "a mixture of maternal overprotection and maternal rejection" of kids, speaking of "schizophrenogenic mothers." Subsequent research debunked that theory, which one commentator has termed "hopelessly mistaken, and more than a little embarrassing."[11] No, the solution isn't to pass along more blame for something else that isn't their fault. It's to provide parents the knowledge and tools they need to help their kids practice their thinking skills. CPS does that, helping parents to feel *good* about their child-rearing talents once again.

Finally, the notion of *skill, not will* helps parents by making it easier for them to empathize with children and build healthier, more positive relationships. By understanding that their challenging kids can't help their behavior—that these kids lack the skills to comply with our requests—parents can come to see their bad behavior not as insubordination but as a manifestation of their inner struggles. One father told a colleague of mine that after learning about CPS, he realized that his "autocratic, Plan A" way of responding wasn't working. His two boys not only weren't developing the skills they needed to manage their behavior, they also weren't "feeling heard or connecting to [him] as a parent." As this father noted, "I came to appreciate how much of what I saw as strong and decisive and structured [about my parenting] was . . . modeling a lack of empathy or interest in their needs." He resolved to feel more empathy for his kids and their needs going forward.

Even with kids who severely misbehave or act out, a shift in mind-set can transform parents' attitudes. You'll recall from chapter 3 that Jamison Booker behaved so poorly that he made family life "a living hell," as his mother, Marlene, put it. After six months spent learning and practicing CPS, Jamison's behavior had improved, but he still had a long way to go. Still, as his father, Bob, told my colleagues and me, just coming to understand that Jamison wasn't misbehaving willfully—that he struggled with a skills deficit—made a difference. Bob used to feel "anger and frustration," thinking to himself, "Goddamn it, why can't this freaking kid abide by the rules of society and follow directions?" Now that anger had largely dissipated. Bob and his wife felt "sad for Jamison in that it's not his fault. The poor guy just doesn't know how to function and deal with life in many ways." Bob estimated that the level of stress he experienced thanks to Jamison was probably about three-quarters of what it had been before the family had learned about CPS. That wasn't earthshakingly different, but given how desperate the family had been, it marked important progress. Bob allowed that it would take time for Jamison to "rewire those neurons." In the meantime, Bob and Marlene had learned to be more patient, to "not take [Jamison's behavior] personally" and not "[interpret] his actions as a direct affront to us." We often see parents' stress levels decrease even before challenging behavior improves, simply because parents have come to see their children in a more compassionate light.

Helping "Regular" Kids to Thrive

CPS may benefit parents confronted with extremely challenging behavior, but what if you're a parent and your kids are typically developing or well adjusted? Can you benefit from using CPS as well? The answer is a resounding yes. Like their more challenging peers, well-adjusted kids have their own unique set of strengths and weaknesses when it comes to skills. But whereas a challenging kid might struggle mightily in a number of everyday life situations, a more typically developing kid might struggle in only one or two areas—and in a modest way, at that. Your son might not be flunking out of school, but you might wonder if he could be applying himself a bit more. Or your daughter might be doing well in school, but you wish you didn't have to work so hard to get her out of bed in the morning. Or with either of your children, you might be satisfied overall with their development, yet still feel a bit worried about the food choices they are making.

Whatever your area of concern, CPS tells you that you have three choices: try to make your child do it your way (Plan A), do it their way for now (Plan C), or work collaboratively to arrive at a solution (Plan B). If a conflict arises that relates to what you deem a problem area, you might choose to work on it using Plan B so that you can solve it in a durable way, while also helping to strengthen your relationship with your child and build your child's skills. Or you might decide in this instance that your child isn't struggling that much and you don't need to pay special attention to the underlying skills. If you just need your child to comply with your wishes, and she has the skills to do so, you might decide to assert your will. Alternately, you might decide to drop your desires and work on the problem another time.

You might wonder if parents of well-adjusted kids really *need* CPS. After all, these kids are already skilled in relative terms, and any disciplinary problems they experience aren't especially severe. Can't parents get away with simply asserting their will when conflict arises? They can, but as I tell parents, they're missing a huge skill-building opportunity. When children already comply well with authority, they have a much easier time jumping into a Plan B conversation and participating. Through listening to the concerns of their parents, articulating their own concerns, and brainstorming solutions, they can develop a number of more re-fined problem-solving skills that they'll need in order to thrive in the adult world.

We adults are expected to comply with authority figures, too. We have to be able to stay calm when conflict arises with bosses, colleagues, or customers, regulating our emotions, show-ing a certain amount of flexibility, and, in many cases, doing what we're asked. But today's postindustrial workplaces require much more than this. On a daily basis, employees and managers in most settings must collaborate with others to solve pressing business problems. Whether it's crafting an advertising cam-paign, designing a legal defense for a client, negotiating a real estate deal, or coming up with a smart IT solution for a difficult client, most adults find themselves working on teams with others and handling conflict as it arises.

Excelling in this environment requires an ability to listen deeply and intently to what other people are saying and to understand their concerns. You have to be able to communicate your point of view and to negotiate mutually agreeable solutions. You have to be able to look at a problem in flexible ways, so as to generate new, creative solutions. Most of us don't master such skills in school. In many cases, we barely achieve passing competency, because schools are not set up to teach advanced problem solving. And most parents don't explicitly practice these skills with their children, either. By engaging in regular Plan B conversations, kids *do* get a chance to practice these skills, and, with time, master them. By using Plan B with generally well-adjusted kids, we're helping to take their skills to a whole new level, setting them up for success as adults.

Parents who harbor doubts about CPS will often say to me, "Plan B sounds great, but, let's face it, it's a Plan A world out there. You have to be tough. You have to know how to lay down the law. By teaching your kid Plan B, you're setting them up for a rude awakening." On the face of it, that seems right. The police officer who pulls your kid over for speeding won't be trying to understand his perspective and empathizing. Nor will his boss when he shows up late for work . . . again. I agree with skeptical parents that it is a Plan A world—*sometimes*. There are moments in our lives when we do have to have the skills to comply with others' wishes, and to make others comply with ours. But these moments represent only 1 percent of our lives. For the other 99 percent, it's a Plan B world. You have to be a good *collaborator*, *empathizer*, and *problem solver* in order to navigate it successfully. Plan B builds those skills in kids (and parents, too).

Driven to Succeed

Skill building is hardly the only reason to try CPS with well-adjusted kids. The most successful adults out there—people with thriving careers and personal lives—don't just have superior problem-solving skills; they are also highly driven to succeed. They don't need rewards and punishments to prod them to work hard. They have an *internal motivation* spurring them on. Wouldn't we all want our children to develop that internal, or intrinsic, motivation?

Research has shown that compelling a person to behave in desirable ways by using punishments or rewards significantly *decreases* a person's internal motivation to keep behaving that way.[12] Overuse of rewards, for example, leads people to become much more interested in getting the rewards, but less interested in the very goal you want them to pursue. Research has also shown that the most effective way of fostering internal drive in others, including children, is to give them a sense of mastery, a sense of control over their environment, and a sense of connectedness to those around them. Plan A—traditional rewards and punishments—doesn't foster any of those elements. You're *taking away* your child's sense of power, autonomy, and control by attempting to manipulate their behavior, and you're not building an empathetic connection with your child in the process. You're certainly not nurturing empathy, because you haven't shown it yourself in the course of levying punishments or rewards.

Plan B, by contrast, fosters a strong empathic bond between parents and children. And by inviting kids to participate in forging a solution, it imbues them with a sense of power and autonomy. As kids become better problem solvers, they feel more competent and want to do more of it. They feel increasingly effective, masters of their own domain, and are driven to engage with others and the external world. Built on the notion of *skill, not will*, Plan B winds up fostering both skill *and* a strong inner drive to learn and grow.

COMMON MISCONCEPTIONS ABOUT PARENTING

"I need to control my children so they respect me and know who's boss."

"Kids are easily spoiled, and if I give them an inch, they will take a foot."

"The world isn't easy. I need to prepare my children for hardship by not giving in."

"If I give up my anger, I give up my expectations for my kids."

"If the child wins, the parent loses."

Relating Better with "Typical" Kids

Parents of typical kids can build much closer parent-child relationships by using CPS and Plan B. Brooke and her husband, Matt, have two kids, including a well-adjusted thirteen-year-old named Thomas. When Thomas was twelve, he asked Brooke and Matt to let him come home from school and spend afternoons without adult supervision instead of having him attend an after-school program. Brooke and Matt consented, as long as Thomas agreed to spend his time responsibly, taking care of certain tasks around the house. They didn't want him to come home and play video games all afternoon. What they did want him to do was to walk the dog, a job that Thomas disliked.

One hot September day, Matt came home to find that the dog's leash was not in its usual place, but in exactly the same place that he had dropped it that morning when he'd left for work. He inferred from this that Thomas hadn't walked the dog. Matt grew angry and confronted Thomas. "You didn't walk the dog today. I know you didn't!"

"Yes, I did!" Thomas screamed.

After a few slammed doors, the encounter was over. A little while later, Brooke went to talk to Thomas. Her first inclination was to lecture him about lying, telling him that he would have been better off admitting to his dad that he hadn't walked the dog and accepting the consequences. Instead, she took a deep breath and resolved not to focus on his lying. She would use Plan B and try to come to a collaborative solution to the dog-walking problem.

"So, Thomas," she said, "it seems like something happened earlier about walking the dog. What's up?"

"It was too hot," Thomas replied.

"I see. There's something you don't like about walking the dog when it's hot. Can you tell me more?"

"No, Mom, it's not that I don't like it. The vet said that if the blacktop is too hot on my hand, it's too hot on her paws. When I felt the road, it was too hot for her."

Brooke's eyes widened. "Oh, wait, so you didn't walk the dog because it was too hot for her paws?"

"I did walk her, sort of. I brought her into the backyard and ran around the yard a bunch of times on the grass so she didn't have to go on the blacktop."

"Ah. Without the leash."

"Right, because I closed the gate. Why would I have put her on the leash?"

If Brooke had applied conventional discipline, she might never have discovered the real reason Thomas hadn't used the leash. She and Matt would have levied a punishment, causing resentment and perhaps leading to future disciplinary issues. By suspending her inclination to assert her authority, Brooke was able to learn valuable information about her son. As she told me, "It turns out that I didn't have a son who was a lying sociopath. In fact, I had a child who was very responsible and who had flexibly solved a problem on his own."

In this case, Brooke didn't have to complete the three steps of the Plan B conversation. All she did was enter the conversation in a neutral way. "That was the day," she concluded, "when I realized that the most important thing Collaborative Problem Solving had done for me as a parent was to change the discourse between my son and me. By entering into conversations with him assuming (or being willing to consider) the best, I regularly avoided the frequent conflict that is common between adolescents and their parents."

As time passed and Brooke continued to apply Plan B with Thomas, she found that their problem-solving conversations were not merely yielding new insights into his behavior but allowing her to broach topics that many parents can't discuss with adolescents. On one occasion, she and Matt grew concerned about Thomas's frequent texting during the evening. Over a period of a few weeks, he got in the habit of burying his head in his phone during dinner and for hours afterward. A Plan B conversation revealed that he was trying to help out a girl at school who had broken up with her boyfriend and was feeling lonely and friendless. This, in turn, led to what Brooke termed "an incredibly rewarding conversation" in which she and Thomas discussed a number of sensitive topics, such as suicide and eating disorders. "Two weeks later," Brooke related, "he reported that his friend was doing better, and that the trouble seemed to have passed for her, something he probably never would have even mentioned to me otherwise."

The Plan B conversation had allowed Brooke a window into the "inner world" of her son's concerns. And what was especially wonderful, Brooke reported, was the increasing ease with which this window was now opening. In some cases, Brooke didn't even have to start a Plan B conversation, because Thomas was beginning to apply CPS on his own. On one occasion, Brooke had agreed to let him use money he'd saved to buy an Xbox video game system. On the day of the purchase, Thomas asked her what games he would be allowed to buy. His friends liked to play certain games, and he wanted to be sure that he would be allowed to play with them over the Internet. The family owned other video game systems, and it had long been established that Thomas and his younger sister couldn't play violent shooting games. Brooke reminded her son of the rule, and thought that this was the end of the matter. An hour later, he approached her, wanting to talk. "Okay," he said, "what are your concerns about me playing shooting games?"

Brooke had to laugh that he was turning CPS back at her. She had no idea that he had picked up the concepts so well. She revealed her concerns: She didn't want him to become desensitized to violence and gore, and she didn't want his younger sister to see or hear the games. Having anticipated her first concern, Thomas had looked up his game of choice on the Internet, and had learned that it contained a setting that would let him play with his friends while blurring out much of the gore. As Brooke recalled, "He made a compelling argument that this particular game was a strategy and war game, which was different from getting desensitized to senseless interpersonal violence."

Brooke admitted that he had addressed her first concern. As for the second, Thomas asked whether he could get the game if he promised to play only when his sister wasn't home or in the same part of the house, and if he wore headphones. Brooke agreed that this seemed reasonable. "Since his concern was that without that game he would be limited in his ability to connect with the friends whom he especially wanted to connect with, it seemed he had led us through finding a solution that worked for everyone. My job was done."

Brooke's experience with Thomas suggests the tremendous progress that typical kids can make in developing problem-solving skills through regular Plan B conversations. Brooke brought Thomas onto her level, and he rose to the occasion. The problem-solving process became a kind of common ground, an opportunity to talk about difficult problems and to establish a strong working relationship based on mutual respect and understanding. Rather than regarding his mother's wishes as baseless or "stupid," Thomas made an effort to understand them, just as his mother had done for him. Home life was hardly *kumbaya*—conflict still arose, and resolving it took time and effort. But the process of resolving it brought Thomas and Brooke together. As any parent of an adolescent can tell you, that's quite an accomplishment. And for parents who worry that their kids will use Plan B on them, remember: You can't use Plan B "on" someone, only with them. As long as your concerns are clearly stated and you make sure the solution addresses them, your child can't take advantage of you.

Healthy relationships of any kind rest on mutual understanding. While you might be able to "get away with" traditional Plan A parenting with well-adjusted children, these children probably don't feel well understood. In many cases, their concerns, thoughts, and feelings go underground—they learn to swallow them so as to bend to your will. Worse yet, they often try to address their concerns or get their needs met in sneaky, unethical, dangerous, or illegal ways. In the course of practicing Plan B, you're letting your kids know that their points of view matter to you. You're also assisting and guiding them to learn new skills. The natural result is a solid, helping relationship, one that leaves your children feeling both empowered and understood.

Plan B for Parents: A Brief Primer

If you're struggling with a challenging child or eager to do your best with a neurotypical child, I invite you to experiment with

Plan B. You apply it just as described in chapter 4, both proactively for recurring behavior issues and in emergency situations when you need to help people calm down and resolve a problem in the moment. It's important not to feel overly rule bound as you apply Plan B. It's a structured process, but you shouldn't treat it like a simple script that you mindlessly use. Know the steps and the techniques as well as the theory behind them, but feel free to adapt them to fit the environment of the home. In particular, correct for the reality that you're dealing with a child here, not an adult. Use language that your child can understand, and organize the Plan B conversation in ways that will help you engage your child productively.

For instance, before you initiate Proactive Plan B with your child, you might want to think and plan ahead to catch her at an opportune moment when she is calm and available—and when you are, too. Many times it's best to hold a Plan B conversation when our children are captive, when we don't have to make eye contact, and when there is some distraction and motion available that don't absorb too much attention so they can still engage in the discussion. For one child that may be the bathtub. For another it might be nighttime when being tucked in, and for a third perhaps in the morning while driving to school or while shooting hoops.

When beginning Proactive Plan B, be especially careful not to put your child on the defensive. It's a sad reality, but unfortunately when we approach our children to talk to them about something, most kids immediately sense they've done something wrong. And experience has taught our kids to expect at least a lecture if not Plan A to follow. So you'll probably need to go overboard, especially in the beginning, to show your child that you are just hoping to understand his concerns or perspective, not to lecture or punish him.

In an effort to get Plan B off on a solid footing, start with a neutral observation, like "It seems like trying new stuff has been a little hard"; or "I've noticed that you've been having a hard time going to bed lately and that you like having some electronics with you at bedtime"; or "It looks like wearing shoes that aren't comfortable really bothers you a lot." Notice how those observations aren't about the behavior we want to stop (e.g., "I've noticed you have been hiding your electronics and not being truthful with us") and don't make assumptions, either (e.g., "It seems like you don't think we should be allowed to tell you what to do").

Once you bring up the issue in a neutral way, ask your child to tell you about her concerns. Say something like "What's up?" or "Tell me about that," or "I'm just wondering what's going on." As we've seen, it is very important not to rush this first step, and to use the four empathy tools described in chapter 4: ask clarifying questions, take educated guesses about the other person's concerns, practice reflective listening, and offer reassurance. In my clinical work, I'm constantly impressed by how surprised parents often are by a child's concerns or perspective. Some examples: a high schooler insisting he should not be in honors classes—not because he thought he couldn't handle the curriculum, but because he wanted to be with the "normal kids" so people wouldn't think he was "a nerd." Or the child whose body odor was driving away his friends—it turned out he was in fact taking showers, using deodorant, and wearing clean clothes, but he wasn't using soap in the shower because he didn't want soap that other people had used touching his body.

How would a parent know those concerns? You wouldn't unless you asked and did a lot of probing using the tools. That's not to say that all concerns are hard to identify. Sometimes the concern will be right there on the surface (for instance, your child wants something to eat before it's dinnertime, and you know he hasn't eaten in three hours). Your child's skills at articulating her concerns, needs, and thoughts help determine how easy or hard the drilling down process will be. Keep in mind with very young children that there are many different ways to communicate concerns and needs. It can be done through play, using characters, drawing, making up stories, or any other creative method you can think of that resonates with the child.

Let's take an example of a child who can communicate fairly well. Eight-year-old Michaela has been "borrowing" one of her parents' smartphones before going to bed, denying she took it, and then hiding it under her pillow. Michaela's mother finds this behavior both mysterious and inconvenient. She has decided to address it using Plan B. Notice how Michaela's mother sticks to the four tools and eventually identifies her daughter's concern:

Mother: We've noticed that this isn't the first time you've hidden one of our phones. Don't worry—you're not in trouble. We know there must be a good reason why. Can you fill us in? (*neutral observation followed by some reassurance and a question*)

Michaela: I don't know.

Mother: Well, think about it for a bit. I'm sure there must be an important reason why. (more *reassurance*)

Michaela: I don't know.

Mother: You're really not in trouble. I just want to understand. (*even more reassurance*)

Michaela: I'm sorry. I'll stop doing it, okay?

Mother: Well, I don't want you to just stop without us knowing why you were doing it. Is it because you are bored and can't find anything to do? (*reassurance followed by a guess*)

Michaela: I don't know.

Mother: Or do you just really like the games you can play on our phones better than what you have on your iPod? (*guess*)

Michaela: Sort of but not really.

Mother: Sort of what—you like our games better? (*reflective listening*)

Michaela: Not really.

Mother: Huh. Okay. Well, that's interesting. So you might like our games better, but you're not sure that's the reason you've been hiding our phones. I wonder why. (*more reflective listening and another question*)

Michaela: I said I don't know!

Mother: Remember, you're not in trouble. Really. Is it something about just having our phones with you under your pillow? (*reassurance and question*)

Michaela: I guess so.

Mother: How come? (*question*)

Michaela: It helps me get to sleep.

Mother: Huh. So having our phones with you helps you sleep. Why is that? (*reflective listening and question*)

Michaela: In case I can't get to sleep.

Mother: So you mean you would have something to do if you couldn't get to sleep? (*reflective listening and question*)

Michaela: No, because that way my brain knows it has something fun to think about if there are scary thoughts in my head.

It may not have come easily, but with a little perseverance, Michaela's mother used the four tools to identify her daughter's concerns. At this point, many parents would start offering suggestions for *how* to solve the problem. Don't do this just yet. You are ready to move on to the second step in Plan B when your child is calm, you have a good sense of her specific concerns, and when you can imagine some possible solutions (although don't voice them just yet, either!). It's sometimes good to move on when you know that you've learned something new through the discussion, like Michaela's mother did. If you do move on prematurely, don't worry. Your solution probably won't work, and you can always start again and see if you were on the right track with your child's concern. In the example above, once Michaela's mother understands that her daughter is hiding their phones under her pillow in order to have something to distract her from scary thoughts about bedtime, she is ready to move on to the second ingredient of Plan B, the sharing of her concerns.

So how do you communicate what's on your mind? My advice:

Do so simply and succinctly. Before embarking on a Plan B conversation about a recurring problem, ask yourself: What is my true concern about? Why do I want my son (or daughter) to act differently? Most concerns that parents have revolve around one or more of four things: health, safety, learning, or how their child's behavior affects others. If you're struggling to clarify your concerns, try running through these four categories. If you find that you're able to identify the type of concern you have, it's time to ask yourself to articulate the concern in more concrete language. As we've found, the heightened detail tends to open up more potential solutions for parents as they think through a problem.

In the example above, Michaela's mother would want to ask herself before initiating Plan B: Why *don't* I want Michaela having my phone at bedtime? The obvious answer is that she doesn't want her daughter to be taking things without asking or lying to her. But it might help for Michaela's mother to spend a little time exploring her own concerns: If Michaela asked me for the phone, would I be okay with her having it at bedtime then? Probably not. Because Michaela's mom might want to use the phone then herself. And she might worry that playing games would keep her daughter up too late. So her concern extends beyond a desire for Michaela to be truthful with her. (And, in fact, I would argue that working hard to understand Michaela's concerns and resolving a problem like this in a mutually satisfactory way would quite likely result in Michaela being more forthcoming in the future.)

Don't expect your child to wholeheartedly embrace your concern the minute you enter it into the discussion. In fact, she may tell you she doesn't care about what is important to you at all. That's no problem: It's your concern, not hers! You each just need to *take each other's concern into consideration*. So if your child says, "I don't care about staying up too late. I'm not even tired!" your response might be: "You may not care about staying up too late, but as your mom I do. That's part of my job. What you care about is having something fun to do if you are having scary thoughts at night, right? And it is really important that whatever solution we come up with helps you with that."

Notice how Michaela's mother reacts to Michaela's discounting of her concern by reiterating the importance of her daughter's concern. In my experience, most kids like Michaela get defensive and dig their heels in because the second their parent shares a concern, the kids suspect that their own concern just diminished in importance. Parental concerns usually trump kids' concerns—something kids learn the hard way. So the mere mention of a parent's concern usually alarms kids. But with CPS, both parties' concerns are important and worthy of being addressed. So if your child reacts emotionally upon hearing your concern, you need to make it clear that you haven't forgotten about hers by going back to the empathy step.

Once you've made it through Plan B's second step, it's time for the brainstorming stage. Ask your child to try her hand at coming up with a solution first. Of course, if your child doesn't have any solutions, then by all means jump in and make a tentative suggestion if you have any good ideas. Just be sure to give your child a chance. Too often kids respond to the invitation to come up with ideas with an "I don't know" after less than one second of thinking. Remind your child to take his time trying to come up with some ideas. And if he can't, think out loud with him. As a good teacher would remind us, share your work! That way, your child will be able to hear how you arrive at certain solutions, and to learn from it.

When you're evaluating ideas and deciding together which to embrace, slow down and encourage your child to think them through with you. Remember the criteria we discussed in chapter 4: Does a proposed solution work for your child? Does it work for you? Is it practical? And does it raise other concerns or cause any other problems? Believe it or not, the actual solution is less important than its ability to satisfy this litmus test. And if your child came up with the solution, all the better.

In the scenario we've been following, the brainstorming step might look like this:

Mother: I bet there is something we can do so that you don't get scared at night, don't stay up too late, we aren't missing our stuff, and you can be truthful with us. Do you have any ideas?

Michaela: I don't know.

Mother: Well, think about it a little bit. It's not an easy problem to solve. It might take some thinking, but I'm sure we can come up with something together. (*giving Michaela a chance, biting her tongue, and offering some optimism and reassurance*)

Michaela: I really don't know.

Mother: Okay. Well, let's think together. Can you think of anything else that you could have that would be fun for you but that we might not need?

Michaela: Yup.

Mother: What's that?

Michaela: Dad's iPad!

Mother: Well, that's one idea. Let's think about it together. (*patiently remembering to help Michaela practice rather than just ruling out the idea right away*) Would that work for you? (*walking her through the litmus test*)

Michaela: Yes!

Mother: And would that work for us?

Michaela: Yes!

Mother: Well, let's see. I suppose we'd have to check with Dad to see if he needs his iPad then. But what about the issue of you staying up too late? (*still helping Michaela test out the solution*)

Michaela: I won't! I promise!

Mother: Well, I know you would try hard not to, but sometimes the games are so much fun that they are hard for you to stop playing. (*helping Michaela test the feasibility of the solution to protect against wishful thinking*)

Michaela: I have an idea! What if you just came up to check on me after a little bit to see if I was using the iPad or not?

Mother: I suppose I could do that. But what if you were using it—what we would do then?

Michaela: You could remind me to put it away, and I could try to get to sleep again.

Mother: And the telling-the-truth part? Do you think you could be honest about things and not try to hide using it from us?

Michaela: Yes.

Mother: I suppose we could try that if you really think it might work.

Michaela: It will!

Mother: I guess I'm hoping that if we can solve problems together like this so it works well for both of us that you won't feel like you need to hide the truth from us. But if this solution doesn't work, I promise you won't be in trouble. We will just have to keep thinking of other ideas together. Okay?

Michaela: Okay. So can we try it?

Mother: As long as Dad is okay with it. And then let's see what happens and we can talk again.

Michaela's mom knows that she's done with Plan B for now because she and her daughter have arrived at a solution that addresses both of their concerns, is possible, and won't cause other problems. They also have a follow-up plan. Notice how Michaela's mom finishes Plan B with an invitation to revisit the problem if the solution doesn't work. A failed solution is a great opportunity for learning. After all, few complicated problems are solved at the first attempt.

If Michaela and her mother's solution ends up working, who wins in that scenario? They both do. Who loses? No one. Michaela's mom accomplishes a number of goals at once. She maintains her expectations for her daughter, reduces challenging behavior, strengthens the helping relationship she has with her daughter, solves a chronic problem so that it doesn't keep arising, and helps Michaela build her problem-solving skills. Pretty cool, right?

When I present Plan B to parents and illustrate it with scenarios like this one, parents sometimes claim that life is hectic and they can't afford to stop and perform the three steps all the time. "Will I have to negotiate over every little thing now?" they ask, as if Plan B will turn their kids into little lawyers. I have to explain that the approach is called Collaborative Problem Solving, not Collaborative Negotiating. You don't problem solve everything. You only problem solve issues that are already problems. Also, you can do Plan B just about anywhere, often in just a few minutes. The car is a wonderful place to do Plan B. Because you're not looking each other in the eye, your child will be less inclined to feel as if you were putting him on the defensive. Remember, too, that Plan B will free up your time. Stealing five minutes in the car or over breakfast in the morning to work through a recurring problem that gobbles up fifteen minutes each time it emerges is time well spent.

> You don't problem solve everything.

Some parents have trouble learning Plan B. Having been raised and schooled in strict, authoritarian, Plan A thinking (as most of us have), it's difficult to break away and embrace a process that stresses empathy, listening, and problem solving. I wish I had a dollar for everybody who sat in my office and said, "Hey, my parents were Plan A and I turned out okay." But when parents learn more about Plan B, they usually warm up to it. Undergoing that shift in mind-set, they regard Plan B as far more than a soft approach. And in the vast majority of cases, they find that it produces much more impressive results.

Raising the Next Generation

Plan B brings an array of benefits to parents. In the short term, parents and kids learn a healthier, more productive, more compassionate way of solving problems. Strife eases, and family members get along better. Over the long term, children improve their skills. They feel better about themselves, become more intrinsically motivated, and develop closer relationships with their parents. But there's an even more profound benefit, one that follows from Brooke's observation that her son Thomas had come to deploy Plan B on his own.

By practicing Plan B with kids, we teach them a radically different way of viewing authority and of solving problems, a method that they can one day pass on to their own kids. And we teach them an underlying mind-set of compassion and collaboration. When parents practice CPS with kids, the kids learn that their concerns, desires, hopes, and worries are just as important as their parents', despite their own relative lack of power. They learn that people can solve problems together in ways that consider everyone's concerns and that don't produce "winners" and "losers." They learn that authority figures can be strong and compassionate at the same time. And they learn that each of us has our own skill struggles, and it's okay to be a work in progress.

Our society does a poor job of raising people to become strong, collaborative problem solvers. As a result, we have become less empathic in recent decades, not more. Adults are feeling less connected with one another, and extremism, divisiveness, and *might makes right* thinking rule the day. Rare is the individual who invites another party to a conflict to sit down and explore their mutual concerns, so that they might arrive together at a mutually satisfactory solution. As parents, we have the opportunity to change this. We can raise a generation of kids who look at authority and the resolution of conflict in a more productive, more compassionate way. Our kids are watching us. They're paying attention to how we behave when conflicts arise. As parents, what do we wish to teach?

CHAPTER SIX

Transforming Workplaces

Mental health professionals are supposed to help people manage conflict and relate better with others. But sometimes professionals don't get along with one another. At one mental health agency, the office administrator, a woman I'll call Cynthia, was clashing with Tammy, the case coordinator whose job it was to organize care for patients. Over a period of months, tensions between the two employees mounted. It got so bad that the two were passing in the hallway without saying hello, withholding information from each other, making sarcastic comments to each other in meetings, and slamming doors to express their displeasure. The office was small—only seven people—so everyone's work was affected.

Typically, a boss in this situation would assess the problem, determine fault, and levy punishments, such as issuing verbal or written warnings. If after a certain amount of time employees still couldn't get along, the boss might terminate or reassign the employees. But that's not what happened here. The office manager—a woman I'll call Debbie—had been trained in CPS and Plan B. Although she had learned Plan B to help deal with the challenging kids whom the organization served, she had also used it for several years with her team to manage conflict as it arose. Now, as conflict between Cynthia and Tammy veered out of control, she invited them into her office and facilitated a Plan B conversation.

Debbie began by prompting each employee to express her respective concern to the other. Cynthia stated that she found Tammy to have an abrasive personality—when asking Cynthia for things, she was often grouchy and frequently rude—and Cynthia deemed her hard to work with and unapproachable. Tammy didn't deny that she could be abrasive, but she pointed out that she had a tough job, and she felt that Cynthia expected her to always be "happy" and "chipper." Tammy was upset that Cynthia hadn't respected her enough to communicate her displeasure to her directly and felt Cynthia should be able to respond to her requests without being so concerned with her tone. For weeks Cynthia had said nothing before eventually complaining to Debbie, their boss.

When all the concerns were expressed, Debbie prompted Cynthia and Tammy to brainstorm solutions. How would the two navigate their relationship moving forward? Tammy was adamant that Cynthia communicate directly to her any problems she might have. That was a nonstarter. Cynthia didn't like confrontation, and she felt uncomfortable complaining to anyone, especially Tammy. Debbie chimed in with a possible solution: What if the two corresponded about requests and issues via e-mail? That way, Cynthia could communicate directly with Tammy, as Tammy wanted, but the technology itself would serve as a buffer, allowing Cynthia to feel more comfortable and lessening the impact of Tammy's brusque tone. Because communication would take written form, both employees would have more time to think through what they wanted to say. Their raw emotions would no longer come through as much in their communication.

Tammy and Cynthia liked the idea, each perceiving that the arrangement addressed her own concerns. They both agreed to try it. Debbie added a clear expectation: There would be no more slamming of doors. No more silent treatment. No more snarky language. No more incivility of any kind. The two didn't have to like each other, but they did have to interact in a professional manner. Is that Plan A, you might ask? No, that's Debbie firmly stating an expectation. If the behavior recurred, Debbie would then have three options for how to handle it.

The Plan B conversation worked. Tammy and Cynthia had come to understand each other's point of view—maybe not perfectly, but better than before. They began communicating more frequently via e-mail, and their uncivil behavior diminished. Because Cynthia had long struggled to express her concerns, the conversation itself gave her more confidence, and she began to speak up more with her colleagues. The e-mail arrangement also allowed her to communicate her concerns and, further, to document them. Meanwhile, Tammy felt more understood and respected. Within a few weeks, the office became more hospitable—everyone noticed it. With less drama to distract them, colleagues were better able to concentrate on their work.

Trouble at Work

Despite more open, collaborative cultures and more attention paid to soft skills, such as relationship building and empathy, organizations still struggle with many of the problems we touched on in chapter 2: rampant workplace conflict, disengaged employees, high attrition, and subpar productivity. According to one study, 70 percent of employees surveyed saw "managing conflict as a 'very' or 'critically' important leadership skill," while 43 percent of employees thought that their bosses didn't "deal with conflict as well as they should."[1] As a result of poorly managed conflict, far too many employees hate going to work, complain about their bosses, and feel little loyalty to their organizations.[2] A conflict-ridden workplace also makes it harder for bosses and colleagues to deliver frank, productive feedback to one another. One 2015 Harris Poll found that more than two-thirds of managers disliked providing feedback to their employees, while more than one-third expressed discomfort about communicating anything that might trigger a negative response from employees.[3]

Why are workplaces so troubled? One reason might be inadequate conflict resolution training. Business schools and corporate training programs offer some exposure to conflict resolution methods, but typically in relation to specific tasks, such as the solving of labor disputes or the negotiation of deals. Most bosses and employees don't study how to handle day-to-day conflict situations with colleagues, customers, and others as they arise. Although countless books and training manuals have addressed conflict resolution in the workplace, they haven't presented a simple, evidence-based approach proven to work in the most challenging of settings that colleagues can apply consistently to solve problems and prevent them from worsening.[4] It's all too easy for bosses, employees, and organizations facing conflict to resort to the traditional discipline they grew up with and have seen practiced in every organization they've encountered.

CPS didn't originate as a workplace solution, but I believe it offers a promising alternative. As Debbie's story suggests, it's applicable to workplaces, and also effective. Simple and easy to learn, CPS provides managers and employees with a common process for addressing concerns, one that much of the time will allow them to come together as equals to design workable solutions. Employees feel empowered and listened to, and managers no longer have to wield their authority at every turn in order to get the results they need. Discussing her ongoing use of CPS with employees, Debbie observes that Plan B "makes everything clearer, including your own expectations," and it is "particularly helpful in getting folks to talk about their concerns. Typically, people [in conflict] hold steadfast to their positions and then bring their own respective solutions to the table, which usually amount to 'I want you to do this differently.'" CPS allows people to talk about their concerns and arrive at solutions that reflect everyone's points of view.

> CPS provides managers and employees with a common process for addressing concerns.

Debbie cites other benefits, such as the predictability of the conversation when a manager uses CPS consistently over time. "Everyone knows exactly what these conversations with me are going to look like, and there is safety in that. They know that any solution [arrived at through Plan B] will meet everyone's needs. It gives them confidence in the process." Meanwhile, Debbie has come to better understand the skills deficits that give rise to challenging behavior. This is "a huge benefit" that lets her understand what is happening day to day, steer her employees to solve problems better, and, over time, seize opportunities to develop their skills. "I know their lagging skills so well," she says, "that I can often anticipate their concerns before they even need to voice them." It's no surprise that in thirteen years only one employee has left her team for reasons unrelated to health or maternity.

My colleagues and I have amassed considerable anecdotal evidence suggesting that CPS gets results in workplace settings like Debbie's. In dozens of schools, hospitals, and prisons with which we've worked, administrators and staff members have applied CPS with one another to handle interpersonal conflicts. The organizations that have done best with CPS all reported an epiphany or turning point in which they realized the value of implementing Plan B as a management strategy to improve teamwork and transform the entire organization. I often tell staff in child mental health agencies that the most important collaborative problem solving they will do will not involve a child. CPS usually takes hold in organizations only once staff have encountered problems in implementing the approach and used CPS itself to work through them.

If you wish to help your team to become more productive,

adaptive, cohesive, and collegial, consider departing from conventional discipline. You can empower your team to address problems that previously might have festered, while helping your organization to create a culture in which people are more understanding of others, more inclined to listen rather than to talk, and more skilled at handling conflict. Much about CPS in the workplace remains unknown, but chances are we can achieve tremendous results there from rethinking how we address conflict. Challenging kids can teach us how to handle conflict in many environments. I'm eternally grateful to them for that. We just have to open our minds and listen.

Employees Change If They Are Able

Michael runs a children's mental health center in Ontario, Canada, with about fifty staff members. When my team checked in with him during the summer of 2016, his organization had been using CPS with kids for nine years and internally as a management model for three years. As Michael told us, his organization hadn't originally intended to use CPS internally, but as time passed it seemed like something they should embrace so that they "practiced what they preached." Staff members had seen dramatic improvements in patient outcomes since implementing CPS. Why wouldn't it work with employees?

Previously, Michael and his fellow managers had handled behavior or performance issues the usual way, by deploying rewards and punishments. Since implementing CPS, the management team addresses conflict by assuming from the outset that skill, not will is causing the problem, and by holding individual

Plan B conversations with employees. On one occasion, Michael facilitated Plan B with an employee who wasn't submitting required paperwork on time. According to regulations, the organization has to submit a treatment plan for each patient within thirty days of an admission. Failure to submit this paperwork could have serious consequences for the organization, as its accreditation depends on it.

This employee was consistently late with the paperwork, although her performance otherwise was stellar. Michael approached her and started Plan B by observing, "We notice that you haven't been getting the paperwork in on time. Why is that?" It turned out that this employee had been slow to turn in her paperwork because she thought it had to be "perfect," and she found it hard to make time to check and recheck her work. Michael and the employee arrived at a solution whereby she would do her best to commit a treatment plan to paper and then have a colleague review her work. If the colleague's review was favorable (it usually was), the treatment plan would be turned in as is. This way, she could hand in the paperwork on time, and her concerns about its quality could be allayed.

As Michael made clear, he and his team don't use Plan B exclusively. Sometimes traditional discipline (Plan A) is necessary, and it is there if they need it. However, "we shy away from the traditional route. Our first attempt to resolve a problem is through skill, not will, and a collaborative conversation." Michael estimates that his organization uses Plan B as a problem-solving process about once a month, or more frequently if a staff member is facing significant challenges. Like parents practicing Plan B with kids in the home, Michael and his managers often find that Plan B uncovers and addresses employee concerns they didn't know about, such as employee confusion about the level of quality required on paperwork. Much of the time, he finds that managers can solve problems by working on them collaboratively with staff, in many cases preventing the organization from having to censure or terminate an employee. Although Plan B conversations take time, he is confident that they save the organization money, given the high costs that accrue when an organization terminates an employee and must rehire, as well as the costs that pile up when problems go unsolved and recur.

Analyzing Michael's story, we find once again that CPS is essentially a two-part management tool: the *mind-set shift* and the *specific problem-solving method* of Plan B. As Michael related, his team's most basic move was to shift their mind-set, discarding the notion that bad behavior at work stemmed from problems with attitude or motivation. "The traditional way of looking at employees is [to believe] that some are great and others aren't motivated to work hard," Michael said. "After using CPS, I think that this is completely flawed. Our staff who do well with our patients have the skills required to pull it off without much effort. Those that struggle are equally motivated. If they could do better, they would."

Instead of jumping to the assumption that an employee is careless, disrespectful, thoughtless,

Remind yourself that, just like kids, your employees or colleagues all *want* to do well.

entitled, lazy, or just plain mean, try assuming the best. Feel empathy for the person, even if you find his behavior objectionable, intolerable, and unacceptable. Remind yourself that, just like kids, your employees or colleagues all *want* to do well. "I bet Bob would prefer to be on time for his two p.m. meeting," you might tell yourself. "I'll bet he'd love to say things that ingratiated himself with the team instead of alienating them. There must be something that is getting in his way, maybe a challenging situation in his personal life, or maybe an underlying skills deficit."

In recent years, researchers have confirmed the usefulness of empathy and compassion in business contexts. Ernest J. Wilson III and his colleagues at the Annenberg School for Communication and Journalism at the University of Southern California found that across the world's industries, empathy was the "emotional foundation" and "attribute-prime" of successful businesses executives.[5] Research by Gabrielle S. Adams of the London Business School has found that empathizing with a perceived wrongdoer in the workplace can help colleagues avoid misunderstandings and help resolve conflicts before they have a chance to escalate. Managers who foster empathy can "improve workplace conditions."[6]

The specific notion of *skill, not will* is not entirely foreign to workplaces, either. Human resources departments consider skills and "competencies" in the course of hiring and promotion. When employees fail to perform on the job, bosses frequently acknowledge a lack of skill as the culprit, saying, "He just wasn't ready for the promotion," or, "He didn't have the right background or experience." Of course, the skills in question are usually intellectual or technical skills—a facility with certain software programs, say, or knowledge of accounting, or basic math literacy—rather than problem-solving skills. We need to broaden our understanding of the skills that affect employee behavior and performance. At the same time, we must augment the empathy we feel for employees who struggle with such skills and the sense of responsibility we feel to participate in problem solving.

Some precedent exists for acknowledging the relevance of problem-solving skills in the workplace. Many managers know about "emotional intelligence," and, specifically, author Daniel Goleman's theory that people possess skills and traits that affect their success in relationships at work, which he articulated in his influential book entitled *Emotional Intelligence: Why It Can Matter More Than IQ*.[7] This theory doesn't account for the full range of problem-solving skills, though. Goleman discusses social awareness and emotional regulation skills, but he doesn't focus on many other abilities related to communication and executive functioning. Further, the impact of Goleman's theory on conflict resolution in the workplace has been limited. Although many bosses and employees accept that people's social skills influence their performance at work, they still regard behavior and performance as fundamentally a matter of will, not skill. Emotional intelligence may have become part of corporate parlance, and companies may be starting to incorporate emotional intelligence assessments into their hiring and promotion,[8] but they haven't deviated much from rewarding and punishing employees in an attempt to motivate better behavior. It is the rare organization that looks at emotional skills with a growth mind-set, seeing them as capabilities that can be nurtured and developed.[9]

If you take nothing else away from this chapter, remember

this: In the vast majority of cases, *people don't misbehave at work on purpose*, but rather because of underlying skills deficits. Whether or not you regularly use Plan B, as Michael and his team do, shifting your mind-set will transform your workplace experience. You won't take it so personally the next time a colleague disappoints or disrespects you. You'll also behave more humanely toward employees who report to you. You'll show more compassion for yourself, recognizing that your awkwardness around communicating with your boss, say, or your difficulty staying calm with another employee, may just be your own skills deficits peeking through. You won't excuse yourself for disappointing performance, but you'll be in a position to address the root causes—without castigating yourself for "screwing up." You'll remember that *you* would do well if you could.

As time passes, you'll also start to appreciate the diversity of skills that exists on any team—the presence of people, for instance, who lack organization skills but are amazingly flexible, creative thinkers, or who are inflexible thinkers but keenly attuned to others' emotions. And you'll begin to see how one person's strengths can help balance out another colleague's weaknesses (e.g., your colleague who is a rigid but organized thinker can help you, a more creative and flexible but disorganized person, stay on track and deliver an assignment on time and as promised). We're all different, and we can all help one another perform better, for the greater good of the team. The more conscious and accepting we are of our respective weaknesses, the more we are able to fill in the gaps for one another when someone is struggling.

You're Not Too Busy to Solve Problems Collaboratively

As essential as the general mind-set shift is, getting the most out of CPS in the workplace also requires applying the approach well as a problem-solving method. Many managers and teams would object that they are time pressed as it is—how could they possibly devote time and energy to resolving disputes collaboratively? I've heard that in every organization with which we've worked. Nobody has time. Why not? Because they're constantly dealing with the Groundhog Day Effect—waking up to the same chronic problems day after day.

Imagine if, thanks to constant practice, others on your team were as well versed in Plan B as you are, able to solve problems with their colleagues as they arise. Imagine, too, if any skills deficits they had were improved, thanks as well to all the on-the-job practice. All of a sudden, you'd have a lot more time as a manager. Your team would become more productive, more adaptive, more cohesive, and more collegial. Problems that once festered would now be addressed. People would be more understanding of others, more inclined to listen rather than to talk, and more skilled at handling conflict situations. The whole environment of your workplace would change, as would your business performance.

How exactly should bosses apply CPS? Some urgent situations demand Plan A. When it's the day before the big presentation and team members disagree about how to frame a particular point, there may not be time for a lengthy conversation. You as the boss need to make an executive decision and dictate a solution. But these situations are truly the exception. Most of the time, bosses have more flexibility in how they respond, and their imposition of will primarily serves to alienate and disempower employees. Employees might go along with the boss's decision because they feel they have no choice, but inside they feel angry, resigned, and unmotivated.[10] Because the underlying cause of the problem hasn't been addressed, the problem will likely continue to arise. And when it does, employees won't know how to resolve the problem themselves, as they've been relying on their boss to do it for them.

As for Plan C, managers do need to pick their battles—they can't resolve every problem or address every strategic decision immediately. But if they resort to Plan C too often, staff might see them as weak or as unwilling to address the underlying issues. And the problem will linger. Plan C, remember, is a strategic choice to handle a problem at a different, more opportune time or to prioritize. You can't work on everything at once. Managers should use Plan C tactically, remaining mindful of their priorities and of their limited time.

Plan B gives bosses and subordinates a structured and predictable way of working out conflict *together*, despite the power disparity, and of addressing strategic questions collaboratively. Colleagues can use Plan B conversations preventatively—Proactive Plan B—to handle recurring problems, or spontaneously to respond to a crisis situation—Emergency Plan B. Like Debbie in our opening story, managers who become skilled at CPS won't need Emergency Plan B very often. They can fall back on solutions generated from previous proactive conversations.[11]

THE THREE PLANS: WHICH TO USE?

YOU MIGHT USE PLAN A WHEN . . .

➤ You have a tight deadline and a decision simply needs to be made.

➤ You need to make a statement about your authority and/ or the team or organization's vision.

➤ An employee is taking action inconsistent with the organization's business interests.

➤ An employee is taking action that is blatantly unethical or illegal.

YOU MIGHT USE PLAN C WHEN . . .

➤ You face a deadline situation, there just isn't time to apply Plan B, and you can let the employee choose the solution without grave consequences.

➤ An employee has a concern that is important to her, your countervailing concern isn't nearly as significant in your mind, and you feel comfortable dropping your concern.

➤ You're trying to build up your employees' confidence and want to prevent the appearance that you're nitpicking or micromanaging.

➤ You're managing an employee who is also a manager, and you don't want to subvert her authority in public.

> ### *YOU MIGHT USE PLAN B WHEN . . .*
>
> ➤ You face a recurring issue with an employee, you have significant concerns of your own that you don't feel comfortable dropping, and you don't think Plan A is going to solve the issue.

Holding Better Meetings

In introducing CPS as a problem-solving process for workplaces, I've so far considered the situation in which two professionals are solving problems together individually or with the help of a supervisor. In many cases, members of an entire team have issues with one another or are called together in a meeting to solve a problem that they collectively face. In this situation, managers can use a variant of Plan B—what my colleagues and I call Group Plan B—to make meetings far more productive and satisfying.

Group Plan B is a more structured version of the brainstorming sessions that you often see in companies and other organizations. There are two basic steps. You first go around the room and offer each member of the group a chance to articulate her concerns about the topic at hand. Everyone agrees to voice only concerns, *not* solutions to the problem. Only when everyone has had a chance to express her perspective does the leader invite the group to engage in collective brainstorming.

I have often taught Group Plan B to teachers and caretakers

in schools, group homes, and other facilities, and we've used Plan B to structure group meetings in high-acuity cell blocks in correctional facilitates. We so often assume that bosses are responsible for coming up with the solution. Isn't that what they're getting paid to do? Actually, no: The boss in most cases can make much more headway by serving as a facilitator (much as Debbie did in this chapter's opening story) rather than as the decider.[12]

By using Group Plan B, the boss can create a space for problem-solving conversations to occur, while also offering a clear, simple, and predictable format for the conversation that ensures that *everyone's* perspective is heard and valued and that team members can replicate on their own. Let's say you run a sales team, and your quarterly results are running 5 percent below your goal. Economic conditions are good, and other sales teams in your organization are exceeding their goals. Your team has a strong product to sell. So the problem somehow has to do with your team, its processes, or its strategy. But what is it exactly? You might have your own opinions—perhaps you think the strategy and processes are fine, but certain members of your team are unfocused. Rather than simply making an executive decision to bear down on those individuals or take other action, try initiating a Group Plan B discussion. Raise the issue of the subpar results and ask your team members what *they* think is going on. Have everyone articulate his concerns about the group's performance and what might be weighing it down. Facilitate the discussion, but don't dominate it with your own ideas. Do any of the concerns raised by your team members surprise you? When everyone has had a say, brainstorm solutions that take everyone's concerns into account, including your own. Most of the time, the solution arrived at using this method will be more complete, thoughtful, and creative than any you might have thought of on your own. And perhaps even more important, the whole team will be much more invested in enacting the solution and making sure it succeeds now that they have helped to co-author it.

GROUP PLAN B

THE BASIC PLAN B STRUCTURE APPLIED TO CONVERSATIONS WITH GROUPS OF PEOPLE INSTEAD OF INDIVIDUALS . . .

➤ Is useful for problem solving as well as general brain-storming.
➤ Allows everyone to feel heard.
➤ Prevents the leader from dominating.

Some bosses might doubt that team members can generate valuable solutions largely on their own. When I lead kids through Group Plan B, I'm constantly surprised at the ingenious solutions they present. In one case, I sat with a group of about twenty elementary school students to talk about the challenge they had making a calm, orderly transition between two class periods. The teacher had the kids line up before leaving the classroom, but the kids had a hard time doing that—they would shout and laugh loudly, pushing and shoving one another. During our Plan B conversation, the kids related that they didn't like lining up and standing there for a few moments while waiting for their classmates. Because their bodies were so close together and they were fidgety from having sat in class for the past hour, it was hard to avoid pushing and shoving.

I put it to the students this way: How could they accomplish what the teacher wanted (to get the students from one spot to another quickly, quietly, and safely) while also accounting for their own concerns (having enough room and not getting pushed and shoved)? During the brainstorming phase of Plan B, one child raised his hand. Pointing to the linoleum floor, which had big squares of black and white, he said, "Well, why do we have to be in a line, anyways? Why can't everybody just get a square? We can even put little signs in masking tape on each square saying which one belongs to which student. When it's time to line up, we can each go to our square and we have to stay in our square so that our bodies don't have to touch while we're waiting to leave."

Brilliant, right? The teacher hadn't come up with it. A student had—and it worked. If a group of eight-year-olds can generate innovative solutions, so can a group of twenty-six-year-olds—or forty-six-year-olds.

In many workplaces, brainstorming fails to live up to its potential. As one scholar summarized, "Decades of research have consistently shown that brainstorming groups think of far fewer ideas than the same number of people who work alone and later pool their ideas."[13] One reason may be because participants jump right into proposing solutions before the group has had a chance to define and explore the problem. As Albert Einstein famously knew, problem solving is almost entirely about defining a problem and the different ways of looking at it. If you do that well—if you fully understand the perspectives people have and are committed to honoring all of them—the solution will usually follow naturally. As Einstein put it, "If I had an hour to solve a problem, I would spend fifty-five minutes thinking about the problem, and five minutes thinking about solutions."

In the case of the sales team struggling with subpar results, one or more team members might raise concerns about a new trend appearing in the marketplace that is affecting demand for your product. Exploring this concern, you might discover that customers are interested in different features from what they were interested in just months ago. Someone else on your team might pipe up, observing that your product actually has the new features customers want, but that your sales team hasn't been emphasizing it. As a result, customers don't know about your product's full capabilities in this area. If they did, they would *love* the product every bit as much as they have in the past. Pretty useful information, right?

Following the structure of Group Plan B invites everyone into the process, and ensures that the problem is defined fully. The team is more likely to walk away with a solution and feel the satisfaction of having done so together.

Group Plan B seems especially helpful given the struggles that workplaces have around diversity. Many managers want people from different backgrounds on their teams because they realize the value of bringing multiple perspectives to bear. And yet women, people of color, and other traditionally underrepresented groups may not always feel comfortable contributing due to the persistence of unconscious bias. Research has shown, for instance, that men interrupt women at a staggeringly high rate. In one 2014 study, men interrupted their female conversation partners at a rate of 2.1 times every three minutes.[14] By ensuring that everyone's perspective is heard, Group Plan B fosters a strong climate of mutual acceptance and respect, allowing teams to make the most of the diversity that they've worked so hard to achieve through hiring and career development. It's easy to say that you value diversity and inclusiveness, but think of how it might feel to a young person or a woman or a person of color when the boss takes the time to ask *everyone* for her perspective— not just once or twice, but in every meeting as a matter of course—and to ensure that any solution somehow addresses everyone's concerns. The boss is sending a message: "We care about everyone's opinion, no exceptions. We'll make a concerted effort to make sure that everyone has a say, and that we act on what people say."

TIPS FOR HOLDING SUPERIOR TEAM PROBLEM-SOLVING MEETINGS

❑ Prior to the meeting, make your expectations clear: You want to understand the problem, so people should come prepared with as much data as possible to support their positions. Also, participants will be expected to generate constructive solutions, but not until they have heard everyone else's perspective, so that they understand the problem fully.

❑ At the outset of the meeting, remind people of the ground rules (e.g., "First we're going to share perspectives. Only then will we suggest solutions").

❑ Don't deviate from the Plan B structure!

❑ Be open-minded and curious when participants express their ideas. Use the tools of the empathy step of Plan B: Ask questions and reflect what you've heard to clarify. Remember, understanding someone's perspective doesn't mean you agree or disagree. You are just gathering information. Encourage others to do the same.

❑ Resist the urge to dominate the conversation or to interject solutions of your own before everyone has expressed their concerns.

❑ If some participants are dominating the conversation, let them know that you've heard them and invite participation from others.

❑ Don't rush the conversation. Make sure you devote enough time to understanding the problem before you try to solve it, realizing that the more people you have in the room and the more complex the problem is, the more time you'll likely need.

❑ Beware of solutions in concerns' clothing! "It's important that our new brochure has a picture of every department" is a solution, whereas "it's important that our new brochure represents all our departments" is a concern that could be addressed by many possible solutions.

❑ Don't feel that every meeting has to be structured in this way. Try reserving Group Plan B at first for stubborn problems that haven't been solved by the usual kinds of conversations you've had.

Rethinking How We Do Business

You're an employee at a call center for a major financial institution. You receive a call from a customer who is livid that he has been charged a twenty-dollar fee for not making a monthly payment on his credit card on time. The customer insists that he sent in the payment before the due date, but your computer screen shows that it came in two days late. Do you

(a) rescind the fee and apologize to the caller?
(b) refuse to rescind the fee, explaining that it's company policy to assess these fees and the payment came in two days late?
(c) do neither of the above?

Many employees might be tempted to rescind the fee, reasoning that the payment came in only two days late, and it's not worth it for the bank to lose a customer for the sake of twenty dollars. Better to live by the old saying "The customer is always right."

Ah, but is the customer *really* always right? Not from the point of view of CPS. As we've seen, CPS brings parties in a dispute together on equal ground, even if one party wields authority over the other. Parents and kids, police officers and offenders, psychiatric nurses and patients—all have valid points of view that deserve attention. Likewise, CPS teaches us that customers do have valid concerns, but so do the businesses with which they're dealing. One set of concerns doesn't automatically override the other. The most effective solution is usually one that satisfies both sets of concerns, and that customer and company arrive at together, through dialogue.

If asked, the customer might explain that he makes his payment as soon as he receives his paycheck every month. The paycheck comes just a few days before his payment is due, so he cuts it close. In that scenario, a creative solution could be to rescind the fee this time, but also to change the customer's monthly due date, so that it comes two weeks after the customer's paycheck arrives. This would help ensure that the customer's payment comes in on time from now on. This solution would address both the customer's concern that he has been wrongly charged and the company's concern for timely payments.

When you take time to pursue problem solving with a customer rather than assume that he or she is right, great things can happen. I have experienced this firsthand. In addition to offering clinical care to patients and their families, my organization provides training in CPS to organizations around the world. We used to require that all clients come to us in Boston for our highest level of training. A group of our clients in Canada asked if they could have certified CPS experts near them conduct these trainings, so that they didn't have to travel to Boston. We didn't like this idea. We valued the camaraderie created when our trainees gathered together in Boston, and we wanted our trainers in Boston to retain control over what was taught so as to ensure quality.

We could have disregarded our own concerns and given in to our clients' requests, on the grounds that the customer is always right. Or we could have imposed our desired solution, even if we lost clients. Instead, we tried to practice what we preach. We entered into a Plan B dialogue. When we asked our clients about their specific concerns, they responded that it was too expensive to travel to Boston, and so they weren't able to train as many people as they wanted to. We expressed our concerns about relationship building and maintaining the integrity of the training. And then we opened up the conversation to problem solving. Was there a way we could address both sets of concerns? We arrived at an innovative solution: We would create a new category of "master trainers" whom we would authorize to perform these specific trainings in Canada. They would receive extra instruction and stay in constant contact with us, which would allow us to ensure the quality of the trainings. Meanwhile, cutting out travel costs would allow our customers to train more people. We never would have arrived at this solution if we had assumed that the client's point of view automatically wins out.

"The customer is always right" is just one of many pieces of conventional wisdom about organizations—and specifically businesses—that CPS challenges. We've focused so far on the potential of CPS as a problem-solving approach inside organizations, but CPS has a much broader array of implications for how we might better do business together. Space constraints forbid me from exploring all of these implications, but following are a few common beliefs that CPS shatters, or at least brings into question.

Myth: Hire the Best and the Brightest

Maybe, but make sure you also hire people who are strong problem solvers. The best hires are people who make your job as a manager easier. And those are people who can operate independently, who won't always be running to you for direction when there is a problem. But you should go further and also try to find people who are strong in the specific areas of problem solving suitable for your business. If you're hiring for a high-energy sales position, you'll want someone strong in the areas of social skills and perspective taking (empathy). But look a little closer: If the job is relatively unstructured and you expect that person to be a self-starter, you'll also want to hire someone with strong organizational skills. And if the job has new hires reading off a sales script, flexible thinking may not be as much of a priority.

How do you find employees with the desired skills? Companies often apply sophisticated and costly proprietary methods to test new hires' suitability, including personality tests rooted in scientific research. As helpful as these tests may be, they're not enough. Companies should also evaluate job applicants for their underlying *problem-solving skills* during the interview process. In effect, they're missing out on applying the latest neuroscience, which shows that people do differ in their problem-solving abilities and that these differences correspond to underlying differences in their brains.

Neuropsychologists have developed computer- and tablet-based ways of testing neurocognitive skills, such as flexibility, organization, working memory, and other problem-solving skills.

But you can test for them in simpler ways that don't rely on technology or cost anything. One of my staff members likes to give prospective hires a task to complete when they interview for a job with us. She asks interviewees to look at a Microsoft Excel spreadsheet on a laptop and organize the rows in just a few minutes. She's not trying to evaluate their knowledge of Excel. Rather, she wants to understand how they approach solving a problem under some pressure. If they don't know how to complete this task quickly using Excel, what do they do? Are they able to control their anxiety and think about the problem calmly? Can they delay their impulses enough to stop and think rather than just charging in with a half-baked solution? Can they generate resourceful, flexible solutions to the problem? If not, can they communicate their concerns in a socially acceptable way? In other words, can they employ all the skills we've been talking about that make for good frustration tolerance, flexibility, and problem solving?

To illustrate how much more important problem solving is than simply knowing all the answers, here is a recent story from our own organization. One new hire of ours passed this Excel test by calmly thinking about the problem for a moment and then Googling for an answer, demonstrating emotion regulation, flexible thinking, and problem-solving skills. She has gone on to become an incredible asset to our program, in large part due to those skills. In one instance, her administrative manager asked her to analyze whether we should invest in a new learning management system for our certification program. Having been to business school, this employee vaguely recalled how to perform a Net Present Value analysis to determine the potential profitability of the projected investment. Instead of asking for help right away (always an option!), she went home that night and refreshed her memory using books from her old business school class. She was still slightly confused about how to conduct a proper analysis, so she e-mailed her former professor with questions. He responded with exactly the clarification she needed. She performed the analysis, concluding that purchasing the new system would save us large amounts of money while improving the experience of our trainers. Her manager and I were thrilled with her performance. We could focus on other priorities while she completed the task herself. Hiring good problem solvers pays off!

> Hiring good problem solvers pays off!

Myth: Work Is About Getting Stuff Done

Of course it is. But organizations can benefit from taking a broader view and also looking at the workplace as a venue for skills development.

Okay, you might say, but aren't companies already doing that? Amazon created the Career Choice Program, which provides 95 percent tuition remission for employees who choose to continue to develop their skills, whether they choose Amazon as their ultimate career location or go elsewhere. Companies like AT&T have decided to undertake the "wholesale reskilling" of their existing workforces.[15]

The problem is that companies take an overly narrow view in delivering skills training. They pay attention to conventional job skills that seem directly applicable to productivity on the job—communication skills, leadership skills, and so on. They should also pay attention to neurocognitive, problem-solving skills. Just because professionals have made it to adulthood doesn't mean they're finished with learning how to solve problems. We all have strengths and weaknesses in certain areas of problem solving, and the way to make progress is to practice with others, both at work and in our personal lives.

Most companies probably wouldn't think of helping employees develop problem-solving skills. They assume that difficulties with those skill deficiencies are personal and that employees should remedy them on their own. Work isn't a therapy session, they think. It's work! But CPS isn't therapy. It's *problem-solving training.* Training managers and employees in CPS helps individuals and teams get more work done by offering them a powerful way to solve chronic problems. And as we've seen, CPS also helps individuals build their skills in a customized way, which makes them more resilient and better able to handle future conflict. As a result, they're likely more productive, happier, and engaged. By addressing skills development openly, organizations hasten employees' progress. They pave the way for colleagues to respect and accept one another's imperfections, and to help one another grow.

You might be surprised at what happens if you start implementing these ideas at work. That employee who drops the ball on long-term projects might learn better planning skills. That employee who comes in late to work frequently might learn to organize his life better—and be at his desk by eight-thirty. That supersmart employee who stays silent during meetings and doesn't contribute might learn to communicate better—and come through with a dazzling innovation that no one in the meeting would have otherwise suggested. That colleague who tends to rub people the wrong way might learn to consider other people's perspectives better—and behave more empathically toward others.

I've seen the benefits of emphasizing neurocognitive skills development firsthand. One of our new team members was an extremely bright and caring person, but also a rigid thinker. She had her own ways of working, and she found it difficult to try new or different approaches. During a three-year period in which she practiced CPS, she became more flexible and better able to entertain new ideas that contradicted or questioned her existing beliefs. On one occasion, she demonstrated the impressive range of her flexibility when she met with me to discuss her frustrations with her job. As her boss, I had noticed that she wasn't happy, and during our Plan B conversation she told me that she felt isolated in the particular area in which she was working. During the brainstorming phase, this employee came up with all sorts of creative solutions that I hadn't considered. In addition to how it might have impacted her work, this employee's skill building on the job helped us adapt her job to her needs, so that we could retain her as a happy, productive employee.

Work isn't just about getting stuff done. It's also about bettering ourselves and others. It's about learning how to engage better in relationships. It's about practicing how to resolve our differences. Paying attention to these softer elements will make work feel more enriching—and, yes, it will also indirectly enhance our productivity.

Myth: *Difficult Employees Have Limited Potential in an Organization*

Maybe they do, but maybe they don't. You might have an employee who is clearly talented, but who has difficulty interacting with colleagues. Perhaps she flies off the handle too easily. Perhaps she doesn't pay enough attention when others are speaking or jumps down people's throats. Perhaps she's disorganized and thoughtless when it comes to project deadlines. Ordinarily, you might write off such an employee and characterize her ability to move up in the organization as limited. Yes, you might think, this employee is talented, but it would take too much for the organization and for you personally to help her move up. Better to place a ceiling on this employee's future in the organization, or even to usher her out the door.

If you keep CPS in mind, you might analyze this employee differently. As we saw in chapter 5, skills development occurs unevenly. Some of the most challenging kids are exceptionally bright and talented in other ways. As a parent, you wouldn't want to give up on your kid just because she struggles in her interactions with others. You'd want to help build her skills. Likewise, wouldn't it be a shame for you to give up on an exceptionally bright and talented employee simply because she's difficult? Using CPS, you don't have to. During coaching conversations, you might discern that her behavior problems at work stem from struggles with just one or a couple of discrete problem-solving skills. You can retain higher ambitions for this employee, but still deploy Plan B to help her build her skills.

Recognizing that work serves as a venue for honing problem-solving skills leads us to rethink how we develop young employees. A number of management experts and companies have advocated that bosses serve more as mentors, coaches, and facilitators, and less as stern authority figures.[16] But what does this mean exactly? Like organizations in general, bosses who wish to become better mentors should broaden the set of skills they try to develop in their mentees. They should supplement traditional developmental goals, such as learning to manage a business unit in a foreign country, with goals framed around problem-solving skills (i.e., becoming better at perspective taking or reading social cues better).

When you start working with an employee, assess her neurocognitive skills in addition to more traditional workplace skills. Where is the employee strong, and where is she weak? What specific behaviors do these strengths and weaknesses produce? What specific situations or interactions trigger problematic behavior as a result of skills deficits? You can perform this analysis formally once you know a new employee reasonably well by completing our Thinking Skills Inventory (see chapter 7) and asking the employee to fill it out, too.[17] Asking these kinds of questions, you can use Plan B to help individual employees progress in a customized way, thus making the most of the talent at your disposal.

You might feel nervous about broaching neurocognitive skill struggles with employees. Some skill struggles, like an employee's difficulty organizing information, might be easier to bring up than others, such as an employee's difficulty with body language or his difficulty knowing how he comes across to his colleagues. Fortunately, you don't need to talk openly about skill struggles with a person in order to help him develop those skills. As we saw earlier, Plan B builds skills without overt acknowledgment that skill building is occurring. People think they're solving a problem (which they are). Skill building gets "sneaked in" through the back door.

You might also deploy the structure of Plan B when holding coaching conversations with your mentees about their development. Have them first express their concerns (i.e., what opportunities they would like to develop in their jobs or careers), and then articulate your concerns (i.e., the needs of the team or organization). Then collaborate to determine developmental goals that meet all of the concerns. Remember Michael who runs the children's mental health center in Ontario? He holds these kinds of conversations. He has even created an individualized coaching sheet to capture the conversations, documenting both the concerns and the agreed-upon solutions or strategies. To conclude the conversation, supervisors and employees sign the form, signaling their mutual agreement.

COLLABORATIVE PROBLEM-SOLVING WORKSHEET

Employee name: _____

Manager name: _____

Date: _____

Where and when Plan B will take place: _____

_____

_____

Description of organization's expectations:

_____

_____

Description of employee's concerns/perspective:

_____

_____

Description of manager's concerns/perspective:

_____

_____

Potential agreed-upon solutions: (agreed upon by manager and employee, practical, mutually satisfactory):

_____

1. _____

_____

2. _____

_____

3. _____

_____

I once hired a very senior clinician who had incredible passion for the work, but struggled to understand how he came across to his colleagues when they challenged him. After facilitating Plan B with this clinician, I learned that he often felt on the defensive when it seemed as if the other team members were discounting his experience when he first joined our team. In turn, the other team members felt that he wasn't as open to feedback from them when it came to mastering our CPS approach. After understanding and sharing everyone's concerns, we brainstormed solutions whereby our new clinician's experience was valued while the other team members still felt able to provide feedback when it came to learning CPS. I was also able to share with our new clinician my concern about how he was coming across, and he was able to hear the difficult feedback. He even asked that I continue to give him feedback so he could work on this skill moving forward—he really wanted to be a part of the program. Framing this issue as a skill to be developed and listening carefully to everyone's concerns led to a solution, and it made this discussion possible in the first place.

Some of your employees may well be difficult. And their potential in your organization might truly be limited. But difficult people can change, even when they're fully grown adults. As my friend and colleague Dr. Bruce Perry has said, "One of the great things about the human brain is that it is elastic, malleable"—as long, of course, as you provide

> Difficult people can change, even when they're fully grown adults.

moderate, patterned, repetitive doses of good stress as described in chapter 4.[18] Use this elasticity to your advantage, making the most of the talent at your disposal. And provide that good stress using Plan B.

Myth: When Dealing with Complaints, Scripted Empathy Helps

With an angry customer on the line, it's essential that customer service representatives empathize. But not all empathy is created equal. In chapter 4, I described the dangers of drive-by empathy, when a person makes the gesture of empathizing but is interested simply in acknowledging the concerns before moving on to a solution that primarily addresses her own concerns. In many call centers, scripted empathy is a problem: In response to a customer complaint, the rep will launch into an extended monologue in which she expresses gratitude for the customer's business and an apology that the customer is having difficulty. It's a syrupy, manifestly artificial expression of empathy, and its effect on customers is usually the opposite of what is intended. According to one survey, almost 70 percent of respondents agreed that "their customer service experience improves when agents don't sound like they're reading from a script."[19]

The solution isn't to discard the scripts and give reps more autonomy, as some have suggested. Rather, it's to take a middle path: Throw away the script, but teach reps basic techniques and guideposts for listening and expressing empathy, as well as a general structure for how to solve problems collaboratively with customers. Train reps to think of empathy not as an expression of compassion but as a process of teasing out information so that they can truly understand and acknowledge the customer's perspective. And train reps to know that empathy is not the same as Plan C, just addressing the customer's concerns. Once they solicit the customer's concerns and can truly empathize, they should then articulate their own concerns before proceeding to trying to solve the problem collaboratively.

When an irate customer calls a wireless provider's customer service line complaining that her son had been put on a different, much more expensive plan than the rest of the family, the rep should know how to use the four empathy tools I outlined in chapter 4—asking questions, taking educated guesses, listening reflectively, and offering reassurance. "If I hear you correctly," the rep might say, "you had your son on a totally different plan from the rest of the family. So you had no idea you were overpaying all these months." Reflecting back the customer's concerns has a calming effect. But the rep doesn't stop there and just accede to the customer's wishes. "Here's the thing," she might say. "I'm not sure that I can make a change retroactively to your contract. But I want to help and I understand your frustration. I wonder how we can make this right for you. Let's see if we can come up with some other ideas." And like that, the service rep might launch into the third step—collaborating on a solution.

Plan B as a way of handling customer complaints? Absolutely.

Myth: The Best Salespeople Are People Who Can Talk a Starving Dog off a Meat Truck

Talking a good game is part of it. But *listening* is a more important and often undervalued dimension of sales. At their best, salespeople solve problems for customers. As CPS teaches, you usually can't solve a problem until you first understand it. Take time to listen to the other person's perspective, probing deeply into his thinking, asking questions, reflecting his ideas back to him, reassuring him that you understand and value his concerns. In a sales context, listening helps in several ways. It allows you to gather more information, including concerns that might prompt important innovations or alterations in the solution (the products or services) you're trying to sell. You can have all the market research in the world, but to convince a customer to buy, you have to understand why what you're selling matters to *him*. The act of showing empathy also helps customers feel understood, so that they're more emotionally connected with you and, indeed, more inclined to enter into a relationship with you. Finally, empathy calms customers, allowing them to think with the rational parts of their brains and respond better to the logical arguments that you set forth.

Like managers with their team members, salespeople sometimes enter interactions with customers thinking that they must be authority figures who have all the answers. No. Customers have answers, too. Those of us in sales must be good listeners who are genuinely interested in understanding the customer's point of view. And these days, as companies call upon salespeople to build relationships with customers, not merely seal the deal, listening and empathy become even more important. As the authors of one academic research study have concluded, "It is not just the product or service that is being sold that customers value but salespeople's ability to listen carefully to their explicit and implicit needs so that problems can be solved and priorities established between both parties. In essence, effective listening and communication skills are requisite if the salesperson is to create value beyond the product or service."[20]

Solving Problems When You're *Not* the Boss

Just like people who work with challenging kids, organizations can use Plan B as part of a dedicated effort to resolve conflicts and improve problem-solving skills. They can do this with both individuals and among entire teams. Internalizing CPS principles, they can also begin to rethink many other dimensions of how they operate, including sales, hiring, development, and beyond. If you manage other people, try Plan B with your reports the next time conflict arises. If you run an organization, sit down with your senior team and review the list of skills that help people perform better with others. Think about the skills that members of the team (including yourself!) have and areas where they might be a bit weak—both as individuals and collectively. When conflict situations arise, begin using what we call Group Plan B. Instead of falling back on your authority and imposing a solution on the group, work with the group collaboratively to brainstorm solutions and achieve consensus around a plan of action.

I've focused in this chapter on how managers and leaders might use CPS, but you can also employ CPS principles with colleagues at work over whom you *don't* possess formal authority. Imagine that a partner at a law firm—I'll call him Mark—has an issue with computer software that the IT department installed on his new Mac laptop. Mark only recently switched to a Mac and doesn't understand how the software works, so he asks the IT technician for help. The technician offers some cursory instruction, and then, frustrated with Mark's questions, tells him that Macs are self-explanatory. Mark is angry. Although tempted to assert his will by complaining to the technician's boss, he instead tries to empathize with the technician. Taking a step back, he reminds himself that he and the technician are both doing the best they can with the skills they have. They have to work together, and they both have the same goal—for Mark to be able to use this computer program.

Mark calls the technician and asks to speak with him. Although he might not follow the Plan B steps exactly, he calmly explains that he is new to using Macs, and he invites the technician to share his knowledge. The technician explains that he has fifteen more installations to get through before the end of the day so he is feeling strapped for time. The two of them behave respectfully toward each other, and they work it out. The technician offers more support as soon as he is done with the other installations, and Mark salvages a cordial, professional relationship with the technician. He might not be perfectly happy with how the technician treated him initially, but his problem will be solved, and he no longer feels as angry, having understood the technician's predicament. Going forward, the two say hello to each other when they pass in the hall.

Work isn't the only place where we experience what we might call power-neutral relationships with one another. If you look around your everyday life, you'll find these relationships everywhere. We possess no authority over our neighbors, best friends, spouses, or family members. We're not in charge of

strangers we meet on the street, or the customer service representatives we deal with in stores or on the phone. Yet we do have
to resolve conflicts with these people, big and small. As we'll see
in the next chapter, CPS can help us handle all kinds of conflict
situations we encounter in our everyday lives. It also allows us to
have a better understanding of and relationship with the most
important person of all: ourselves.

CHAPTER SEVEN

Getting Along Better in Daily Life

It's not every day that we have the chance to peer into our own brains and see them working. During the summer of 2016, I had such a chance. A couple of colleagues and I flew to Atlanta to visit a quantitative EEG laboratory run by Youth Villages, a nationwide provider of youth services. Quantitative EEG, or qEEG, is a computer-based technology that measures electrical activity in a number of distinct parts of the brain. We can capture that electrical activity in the form of simple, squiggly lines on a chart, but we can also analyze it using computers, identifying patterns in the electrical activity and portraying them using colorful brain maps. Electrical activity thus gives us a window into the functioning of parts of the brain, as well as their interrelationships with one another.

Psychologists often deploy qEEG to help kids, utilizing it as part of a treatment called neurofeedback training. Kids with conditions like ADHD play video games while hooked up to a qEEG monitor (wearing a skullcap carefully positioned and loaded with sensors). The game lets kids see how their brains are working in real time on the screen. By learning to control their brain activity through specific breathing and relaxation techniques, they can do better in the games and succeed at the tasks assigned them. Over time, some psychologists think, they can train their brains to work better by doing something they love—playing video games.

We were in Atlanta because my organization, Think:Kids, was exploring whether we could use qEEG technology to measure progress in changing the brains of kids who exhibit challenging behavior using CPS. Stepping inside the lab, my colleagues and I found ourselves in a relaxing, spalike environment. The lights were dim, soft music played over the speakers, and pleasing aromatics infused the air. Small exam rooms lined the perimeter of the building. I could have sworn I was about to receive a massage (and I could have used one after our hectic travels down from Boston). Instead, I watched as four or five kids who lived at the residential treatment center filed in to receive their neurofeedback training. They were all excited to be there. One of them, a seven-year-old girl, let us watch as she sat down in a chair and got hooked up to the qEEG machine. They affixed to her head a skullcap studded with electrodes. Using a massive syringe, they squeezed translucent goo through tiny holes in the skullcap. This goo was a conducting agent that allowed the electrodes to pick up her brain's electrical activity.

The girl underwent the training. For five minutes, she sat

comfortably with her eyes open as the technician got a resting EEG. Then the scanning continued as the girl was asked to close her eyes for the next five minutes. While she was occupied, the technician turned to me and showed me scans of children taken before and after they had undergone neurofeedback training sessions. He pointed to a mass of black lines on one of the scans and informed me that the child in question had a significant trauma history and now had severe symptoms of ADHD. The black lines indicated areas of his brain that were overactive, the electrical impulses flying around uncontrollably.

I was impressed. "Wow, this is pretty cool," I said.

"Hey, maybe you'd like to try getting scanned yourself."

I glanced at the little girl, who was just finishing up her training, and then at my colleagues and our hosts. "Absolutely. I'm in!"

The girl got up, and I sat down in the chair. The technician affixed the skullcap to my head and injected the goo. I was comfortable in the chair, but as the technician got ready to start the test, I must admit that I felt a bit vulnerable. My colleagues and our hosts were standing there watching. What were we all going to discover about my brain?

For the next ten minutes, the technician took a resting EEG, first with my eyes open and then with them closed. Afterward, he showed me a printout of my brain scans. Glancing at these images, the technician said, "Overall, you look pretty well regulated emotionally. You've got good impulse control, and your thinking looks organized." Good, I thought, nodding smugly at my colleagues. Pointing to the image in the far-right column, second from the bottom—the one with the darkened, filled-in pattern—the technician said, "Wow, now, there you go. Looks like you have a pretty overactive brain. I've never seen one like this!"

"Overactive brain?"

He gazed at the readout. "Yeah. Look at all that activity. Normally, I would suspect that you had really severe ADHD based on this reading, but the rest of this scan isn't consistent with ADHD. Basically, your brain is being bombarded with tons of information all at once." He glanced at my colleagues. "Do people ever say to you that they wish you could just sort of slow down?"

One of my colleagues cracked a smile. I did hear that a lot. Friends and family members told me all the time to slow down, relax, turn my brain off, stay rooted in the present moment. At work, colleagues complained about a seemingly related concept— my distractibility. During meetings, they observed, I couldn't pay attention for more than a few minutes before I began to fidget, text, or check e-mail. As I've tried to explain, I wasn't trying to be rude. I actually was paying attention to what they were saying, but I was also paying attention to five or six other things at the same time. I was generally capable of doing that, even if on occasion I did forget a point a colleague had made. I just find it extremely hard to do one thing at a time, and only one, for very long. I can't bear to sit still for more than a few minutes. I get antsy.

The scan confirmed that what I was experiencing wasn't distractibility per se. I *was* paying attention. But because of the speed with which my brain was moving, I was simultaneously paying attention to other stimuli, too. I might have wanted to focus only on what someone was saying because I found it interesting, but I was forced to contend with a number of other thoughts bouncing around my head at the same time. In more technical terms, the scan had turned up a shortcoming in my information-processing skills—how my ability to attend to a single input could be overwhelmed by all the information coming at me. On the other hand, my overactive brain helped me. Because it led me to multitask, I tended to get more done than if I was performing only one task at a time.

It was illuminating and not too nerve-wracking to compare notes on my brain with my colleagues. I left the lab thinking that for the most part I didn't want to change my brain's makeup, although I did wish I could correct for it in situations where I was expected to focus uniquely on what others were saying. I also wished that I could slow my brain down at times when I didn't need to get stuff done when it would be nice to just relax. There were skills, in other words, that I needed to build.

Weeks later, when I was back in Boston, I found myself thinking more deeply about the scan and what it meant. Although I've devoted my career to talking about neurocognitive skills with people, I hadn't quite come to grips with my own neurocognitive strengths and weaknesses. For years, I had chastised myself for my forgetfulness, for not always listening, and for my habit of multitasking. I knew that these tendencies bothered people, and I felt bad about that. I tried hard to slow myself down and stay in the present moment, but it was tough, and all too often, I had failed. After the brain scan, I felt better about myself. I had known intellectually that my behavior wasn't something I intended. But I hadn't internalized that it reflected my skill struggles and the underlying working of my brain. Now, thanks to the scan, I had.

I showed the scan to my friends, family, and colleagues. Looking at the images and hearing how the technician interpreted them, they, too, understood my behavior better. In their eyes, I was no longer someone who didn't care enough to pay full attention. They understood now that I *wanted* to sit still and pay attention to a single stream of conversation, but that because of the way I was wired, I had a much harder time doing that than most people. Those around me didn't like my behavior any better than before, but they could at least empathize with me better. That change of perspective made a difference. In a small but significant way, it improved my relationships.

Prior chapters have examined the usefulness of CPS in situations where authority figures are confronted with challenging behavior. We've described how parents, teachers, psychiatric facility staff, school safety officers, and bosses do better when they listen, empathize, and collaborate rather than impose their will on the less powerful person. Yet the potential applications of CPS are actually much broader than this, extending into every corner of our lives. I've argued for more compassionate treatment of those who wound us with their behavior, but let's not forget to be compassionate with ourselves, too. Embracing the *skill, not will* mind-set, we can stop blaming ourselves for our own behaviors that we might not like, as well as life experiences that we might find

> Let's not forget to be compassionate with ourselves, too.

hard to accept. Further, Plan B allows us to manage conflict with people over whom we *don't* wield formal authority, including romantic partners, friends, neighbors, and even perfect strangers. More than just an approach to use in our professional and parental roles, CPS can help us get along better day to day—and even minute to minute. Ultimately, it's a way of interacting with the world, a disciplined approach to addressing every kind of challenging behavior in every context.

Seeing Yourself Differently

Although the qEEG map of my brain activity helped me gain a healthier perspective on my own behavior, you don't need access to technology to apply the *skill, not will* mind-set to yourself. There are much simpler ways to become more aware of your neurocognitive skills—where you're strong and where you're weaker. Let's try a quick assessment of your skills that you can perform yourself.

The following list brings together the primary neurocognitive skills described in chapter 2—the ones we use at Massachusetts General Hospital in our assessments when using CPS. This measure has been empirically validated by our research and evaluation team; we know that it accurately and reliably measures these skills. As such, it provides a simple and cost-free way to quickly evaluate a person's problem-solving skills.[1] Take some time to run through this list and rate yourself on each item. Be as honest and thoughtful as you can.

Thinking Skills Inventory (TSI)

How did you do? Did you find some skills that were extremely strong or weak, or did you find only marginal differences? Were you stronger or weaker in certain skill areas? To supplement your own evaluation, run this list by a couple of people in your life whom you trust and who know you well. You want to choose people who you believe will give you useful feedback in an empathic, caring way. Do these individuals spot weaknesses that you have missed? Can they cite examples of situations in which these weaknesses turn up and lead to problems? Make sure that you also ask these individuals to help you identify areas where you're strong.

Now look at your list of skills. Taking into account the feedback you received from others in your life, circle all the skills where you struggle. These are your skill struggles. Just knowing that can help you think differently about your life, like it did for me. Ask yourself, to what extent and under what circumstances do these skill struggles prevent you from achieving the goals you set for yourself or from living up to others' expectations? And are there ways in which your skill struggles are also advantageous for you? Again, my skill struggles related to my "overactive brain" cause friction with others, but they also help me in my work. You will likely find a similarly mixed picture as well.

Of course, you might also find that some of your skill struggles are more clearly unhelpful to you. They might have caused you all kinds of difficulty in the past. They might have even cost you relationships and career opportunities. You might have been disparaging yourself for years for behaviors related to these skills. Isn't it

LANGUAGE AND COMMUNICATION SKILLS	CONSISTENT STRENGTH	SOMETIMES A STRENGTH	DEPENDS	SOMETIMES DIFFICULT	CONSISTENTLY DIFFICULT
Understands spoken directions					
Understands and follows conversations					
Expresses concerns, needs, or thoughts in words					
Is able to tell someone what's bothering him or her					

ATTENTION AND WORKING MEMORY SKILLS	CONSISTENT STRENGTH	SOMETIMES A STRENGTH	DEPENDS	SOMETIMES DIFFICULT	CONSISTENTLY DIFFICULT
Sticks with tasks requiring sustained attention					
Does things in a logical sequence or set order					
Keeps track of time; correctly assesses how much time a task will take					
Reflects on multiple thoughts or ideas at the same time					
Maintains focus during activities					
Ignores irrelevant noises, people, or other stimuli; tunes things out when necessary					
Considers a range of solutions to a problem					

EMOTION AND SELF-REGULATION SKILLS	CONSISTENT STRENGTH	SOMETIMES A STRENGTH	DEPENDS	SOMETIMES DIFFICULT	CONSISTENTLY DIFFICULT
Thinks rationally, even when frustrated					
Manages irritability in an age-appropriate way					
Manages anxiety in an age-appropriate way					
Manages disappointment in an age-appropriate way					
Thinks before responding; considers the likely outcomes or consequences of his/her actions					
Can adjust his/her arousal level to meet the demands of a situation (e.g., calming after recess or after getting upset, falling asleep/waking up, staying seated during class or meals)					

COGNITIVE FLEXIBILITY SKILLS	CONSISTENT STRENGTH	SOMETIMES A STRENGTH	DEPENDS	SOMETIMES DIFFICULT	CONSISTENTLY DIFFICULT
Handles transitions; shifts easily from one task to another					
Is able to see shades of gray rather than thinking only in black-and-white					
Thinks hypothetically; is able to envision different possibilities					
Handles deviations from rules, routines, and original plans					
Handles unpredictability, ambiguity, uncertainty, and novelty					
Can shift away from an original idea, solution, or plan					
Takes into account situational factors that may mean a change in plans (Example: "If it rains, we may need to cancel the trip.")					
Interprets information accurately/avoids overgeneralizing or personalizing (Example: Avoids saying "Everyone's out to get me," "Nobody likes me," "You always blame me," "It's not fair," "I'm stupid," "Things will never work out for me.")					

SOCIAL THINKING SKILLS	CONSISTENT STRENGTH	SOMETIMES A STRENGTH	DEPENDS	SOMETIMES DIFFICULT	CONSISTENTLY DIFFICULT
Pays attention to verbal and nonverbal social cues					
Accurately interprets nonverbal social cues (e.g., facial expressions and tone of voice)					
Starts conversations with peers; enters groups of peers appropriately					
Seeks attention in appropriate ways					
Understands how his or her behavior affects other people					
Understands how he or she is coming across or being perceived by others					
Empathizes with others; appreciates others' perspectives or points of view					

refreshing to realize that these un-helpful behaviors of yours actually reflect brain differences in the form of skills deficits? You're not a bad person. You're simply a person with skills to work on. Like all of us.

Try sharing your newfound insight about your behavior with others in your life. Let them know that you're aware of your skill struggles, and that they shouldn't think you are purposely trying to disrespect, hurt, or annoy them with your behavior. But don't stop there. Pick a few skills on which to work. If these skills seem helpful in some circumstances and harmful in others, work on developing the skills in the circumstances where the skills deficit is causing you problems.

I find my tendency to multitask especially bothersome when I'm out for dinner with friends and everyone expects me to focus on a single stream of conversation. So in that context, I can practice putting away my phone and focusing, recognizing that it might be a bit uncomfortable for me. The key to skill building, as we've seen, is *practicing the skill in real life*. Each time I do this, I try to go a little bit longer without pulling out my phone or fidgeting: a tolerable dose of good stress. I might also let my dinner companions know that I'm working on this skill so that they don't feel quite so offended when I reach my limits, become antsy, and revert back to multitasking. Even better, I might let my companions know that I simply need to move around a little to ease my overactive brain. If I keep exposing myself in this way

> You're not a bad person. You're simply a person with skills to work on. Like all of us.

to situations that I find challenging (i.e., situations in which others have expectations for my behavior that my skills don't fully support), then I'll improve little by little.

With any skill struggle, pay close attention to the situations in which your weakness causes difficulty. Are there ways you can practice your skills in advance? For instance, if you know that you have difficulty with time management, and you know that you've got a series of big job interviews coming up for which you absolutely have to arrive on time, you might try consciously practicing this skill at home, when you're surrounded by family members or good friends. Look for situations at home where you are called upon to keep track of time, and where sometimes your difficulty doing so causes friction, and practice there. That way, by the time your job interviews come up, you'll be better able to handle them.

Likewise, if you know you're weak in a skill, you can prepare in advance by problem solving for it. In other words, you can do Plan B with yourself! If you have a hard time managing your time, then make a plan for how you'll handle that during your month packed with job interviews. Maybe you'll schedule fewer commitments of other kinds that month, and fewer on the same days as your job interviews. Maybe you'll set more alarms on your phone to help remind you when to finish up other tasks so that you have time to get ready for and travel to your interviews. If you're like one friend of mine, maybe you'll set yourself the goal of arriving at the interviews an hour early. That way if you're running a half hour late due to subpar time management, you'll still be early. And you'll have an extra half hour to clear your mind, relax, and focus.

A combination of awareness, practice, accommodation, and problem solving can help you address skill struggles over time. But most fundamentally, it can help you *think differently* about your own challenging behavior. If you see your challenging behavior as a character flaw, something you can't fix, you'll feel bad about yourself and you won't take any action to fix it. You'll simply give up, plodding along in the same way as you always have been. But if you see your challenging behavior for what it really is—skills to be developed—you'll put yourself in a position to mend relationships with others and to develop as a person.

Changing How We See Others

Ted, met his wife, Michelle, when they both were in their mid-twenties.[2] They had a daughter, Angie, together. Ted wanted to have more kids, but although Michelle loved being a mom, she decided that she was done—she didn't want a large family. As Angie got older, Ted's relationship with Michelle began to sour. He grew more religious, and Michelle, who had always been an atheist, became more rooted in her beliefs. As Ted observed, he also became more "traditional, more conservative," while his wife became more liberal. As the years ticked by, conflict between the two flared up more frequently. "I think we both got entrenched in our egos," Ted says. We got stuck. Relations between us sort of got ground down." After fourteen years, when Michelle was thirty-nine, the two split up. Their divorce agreement provided for shared custody of Angie.

In many cases, divorce can prove to be not the end of conflict but the beginning of a new, even more contentious phase of it. Couples fight bitter, protracted battles, spending fortunes on attorneys. Both parties come away angry and wounded, their families destroyed as well as their bank accounts. Ted's experience has been different. Although he and Michelle were not exactly friends when they separated, they were both committed to raising their daughter in as peaceful and civil an environment as possible. That was smart thinking: Mental health professionals have long recognized that the biggest predictor of how children fare growing up is not whether their parents get divorced or stay together but how they handle conflict in either eventuality.[3] Ted and Michelle worked out their divorce settlement relatively quickly and cheaply through mediation. Afterward, they focused on moving on with their lives and raising their daughter. It wasn't easy, but two years later, Ted had in fact moved on. He'd met a new girlfriend and felt a sense of peace about the failure of his marriage. His relationship with Angie was strong. She was also happy and healthy and doing well at school.

Ted's ability to accept his divorce and adjust to it in a healthy way required a great deal of hard work. When he and his wife first split up, he began experiencing panic attacks. For the first time in his life, he went into therapy and took medication. While these measures helped a great deal, Ted cites another factor that helped as well: CPS. Ted had learned about the approach as part of his work with challenging kids at a residential treatment center. But as he remembers, he hadn't thought to apply it in his personal life, and he certainly hadn't applied it as conflict with his wife intensified. After his divorce, however, he found that the *skill, not will* concept and the structure of the three plans helped him a great deal. It enabled him to understand the failure of his marriage in more helpful ways. He could have a more compassionate view of his wife's failings as well as his own.

Ted remembers struggling with a number of skills during the last years of his marriage, most notably flexibility, emotional regulation, and perspective taking. As he told me, he became rigidly entrenched in his beliefs, and he fell prey to the temptation of dictating solutions to problems. All too often, he had to have things *his* way. Meanwhile, he had trouble controlling his temper. He was constantly irritable at home, and reacted unpleasantly when his wife didn't meet his expectations. For years, he had a hard time understanding his wife's point of view. Looking back on his own skill struggles and how they had contributed to tension with his wife, Ted was able to wean himself from feeling angry at Michelle. Their conflict hadn't been all her fault. He had contributed to it—not because he was a bad person, but because, like everyone, he was weak in certain skill areas. "We all want to do well," Ted says. "Kids and forty-five-year-old guys, too."

But Ted's *skill, not will* perspective also helped ease his anger and resentment by prompting him to see his ex-wife's behavior differently. When she'd behaved in hurtful ways during their marriage, she hadn't been doing it "on purpose," any more than he had. Looking back on it, Ted realizes that his wife had been suffering from chronic depression, and that she probably had been struggling with empathy and perspective taking just as he had. Confronted with his rigidity, she grew frustrated at times and acted out. Quite understandably, she came to distrust him and see him as someone

> Spouses change if they are able.

who wasn't a team player. As Ted now recognizes, spouses change if they are able: "Michelle wanted to do well, but sometimes things got in the way for her." Further, when Michelle acted in hurtful ways during their marriage, she had been pursuing legitimate concerns, even if her actions weren't so helpful. As Ted reflects, "I get now that she had a reason for the decisions she made. She simply had different perspectives on raising kids." With that understanding, Ted sees no reason to remain angry and resentful toward Michelle for what transpired between them. They had both been struggling to do well in life, using the skills available to them.

Ted's ability to feel compassion for his wife instead of anger has led to a smoother, more productive relationship between them in the present. Although they're no longer together, they still have to work together week in and week out to raise Angie. Conflict arises. Instead of rushing immediately into Plan A, Ted finds himself approaching his ex-wife in a more empathic and collaborative spirit. He doesn't always use Plan B in a structured way, but he doesn't need to in order to experience less conflict with his ex-wife. It's enough to simply think *skill, not will* and engage with an eye toward crafting a solution together that addresses all of their concerns. If Ted has any regrets, it is primarily that he didn't interact with Michelle more collaboratively when they were married. He wonders whether the two of them might not have drifted apart quite so far or so quickly as they had. He feels he's now much more self-aware than he had been, and also much more accepting of limitations in people, adults as well as children. As he says, "We all have light and we all have shadow inside us. We have to accept that we're human instead of fighting it." This attitude has helped him in establishing a healthier, smoother, happier relationship with his new girlfriend.

As Ted's story suggests, CPS can help us by transforming not merely how we see ourselves but also how we interpret others' actions. If you're currently experiencing conflict with others, or if you harbor long-standing resentments toward others, reflect more deeply on the concept of *skill, not will*. Think about a person in your life who has hurt you, even someone who has caused great suffering. Try to occupy his point of view. Are there skills on the above list that he might have been (or still be) struggling with? Really ponder this. What might be (or have been) this person's legitimate concerns? If your conflict is ongoing, is there a way to arrive at a solution that accommodates both your and his concerns?

If you find that you're frustrated with many people in your life, then I have another exercise that might help. Think of the three or four people closest to you. They could be friends, family members, or colleagues at work. For each of these people, list the three most annoying or problematic behaviors of theirs, the ones that cause repeated tension or conflict. Perhaps it's your mother's tendency to pry into your business. Or your brother's habitual lateness. Or the tendency of your best friend to fly off the handle. Or your son's habit of thinking only about himself at times. For each of these behaviors, go through the above list of skills and try to pinpoint those where a relevant weakness might be at play. Spending time on this will allow you to take the abstract concept of *skill, not will* and make it more concrete. The next time you experience challenging behavior, you'll remember the skill struggles that you identified in these individuals. Although you might still feel irritated or upset, you'll find that these feelings pass more quickly. You'll move more quickly to a place of calmness, compassion, and empathy.

Of course, it's important to set realistic expectations. I am not suggesting that you will find it uniformly easy or hard to apply a *skill, not will* perspective to people in your life. Some relationships and contexts are more emotionally loaded than others. We can regard the relationships in our lives and the areas of life in which we move as a continuum. At one end are those where our emotions are relatively subdued. At the opposite extreme, we can find relationships or contexts in which we feel intense emotions. Even with a *skill, not will* mind-set firmly entrenched, we'll have a much harder time feeling compassion and empathy for people who have hurt us, and for whom we feel deep negative emotions. In thinking about people in your life and their challenging behavior, be sure to also consider where you'd place them on the continuum. If you can feel just a little more empathy for those who arouse the most intense emotions in you, that's progress.

Solving Problems When the Relationship Is Power Neutral

In addition to helping us to feel more compassion and empathy and to process difficult experiences in our lives, CPS allows us a way to handle conflict as it arises with many people over whom we don't have formal authority. Most healthy relationships in everyday life don't involve a power difference. Neither you nor your neighbor wields authority over the other. You also don't wield authority over your spouse, your friends, and acquaintances, the customer service representatives at your local bank, or the strangers you happen to encounter on the street. You may feel beholden to these individuals, and vice versa, but the power relationship remains neutral or ambiguous. Although earlier chapters of this book have presented Plan B for use in situations where people are in charge, Plan B works equally well in power-neutral situations.

Heated conflict in power-neutral relationships occurs all the time—during road rage incidents, or arguments with your spouse over household chores, or encounters with rude or disrespectful servers or guests in restaurants. When these situations arise, it's hard to get past the emotions enough to conduct a calm, rational, problem-solving conversation. I spend my days teaching and thinking about Plan B, and sometimes even I have trouble.

So what do you do? Try Emergency Plan B. Let's say you're coming home from work at the end of a long day. You live in an apartment building located on a densely populated block in your city, and parking spaces are scarce. But as you turn onto your street, you see one, just feet from your building. Great! You had stopped at the grocery store on your way home, so now you won't have to lug those bags of groceries very far. Tapping on the accelerator, you zoom up and slink your car into the spot before anyone can take it. You shut off the engine, respond to a text for a moment on your phone, and get out of your car. It's then that you notice the woman who lives down the hall from you. She's standing beside her car with the motor running, her cheeks bright red. "I was waiting for that spot!" Was she? You don't think so. You made a point of looking, and there weren't any other cars waiting. You want the spot, but you also would prefer not to alienate your neighbor.

If your neighbor feels wronged, she is likely to be dysregulated. She's thinking low down in the brain rather than with her cortex. Because dysregulation is contagious, you are probably about to respond in kind. If even a small part of you can bypass that urge and remember the first ingredient of Plan B in this charged environment, you can exert a calming influence. In short order, you will both be in a better position to actually solve the problem.

Hostage negotiators will tell you that the *last* thing you want to do in a crisis situation is try to impose a solution, as that will just add emotional fuel to the fire, increasing the odds of a blowup. Rather, they will try to build rapport with hostage takers through empathy. One police website offers the following advice for law enforcement officials in a hostage situation:

> *In many instances, the whole rationale for the hostage situation is so the [hostage taker] can "make a point" or "tell [his] story." Good. If that's what he wants, allow him to freely express his frustrations and disappointments, but don't let venting become ranting or spewing, which can lead to further loss of control. Instead, modulate your own speech style and content in a calming direction.*[4]

Police in hostage situations try to modulate emotions. In essence, they follow the three Rs: *regulate* and *relate* before attempting to *reason*.

If a situation is so inflammatory that you or the other person can't make it through all three steps of Plan B, then don't try to run methodically and thoughtfully through them. When it comes to regulating emotions, the essence of Plan B is empathy. Rather than being curt with your neighbor or shouting something nasty, try to calm her with reflective listening and reassurance. Don't think about the other steps, and don't think about the other two empathy tools of asking questions and hazarding guesses. These tools elicit information. They don't regulate the other person's emotions. Your goal now is simply to do the latter.

Confronted by her anger that you took "her" spot, reflect her thoughts back at her by saying, "I hear you. I get it. You thought you had claimed that spot, and the next thing you knew, there I was." Or offer reassurance: "Hey, listen, I'm really sorry. I didn't think I was taking your spot. This must suck. You were just about to park and all of a sudden, someone's in your spot." If your neighbor says something rude or nasty to you, then respond with: "Listen, I know you're pissed. You don't have to swear at me. I understand why you're pissed."

If you're so upset that you can't think to offer reassurance and perform reflective listening, try at least to remember the basic argument of this book. *Skill, not will* determines behavior. People don't want to behave poorly. When they aren't behaving well, it's because in that moment they *can't*. That neighbor who wants your parking spot might be behaving like a jerk, and that's unacceptable. But there are probably some important reasons *why* she's acting like this—reasons that perhaps have nothing to do with you.

In some volatile situations when you aren't dysregulated, you might be better equipped to use Emergency Plan B. Once when I was out to dinner I came across a couple on the street shouting at each other. The man looked like he was about to hit his companion. I ran up to them, got in the middle, and told the woman to get away. As she ran down the street, the man was shouting at me, "That no good bitch! That whore! She's going to come back here and I'm going to kick her ass!" As the man was smaller than me, I didn't feel he posed much of a physical threat. I thought to myself, *I've got some options. Plan C is not an option. I'm not going to sit by while someone is assaulted. If I use Plan A, I'll be trying to intimidate him into submission. Although I may get away with that, I'd prefer not to go that route.*

I chose Emergency Plan B. I was able to do that only because *I wasn't the one having the fight, so I wasn't dysregulated.* I was thinking clearly, and, as a result, I could help to de-escalate an otherwise fraught and violent situation. A dysregulated person can't regulate another person. But if dysregulation is contagious, fortunately so is regulation.

"Hold on. Whoa," I said to him. "I don't know what she did to you but it sounds like it was bad. Fill me in. What's going on?"

The man shook his fist. "You can't trust women."

"So did she do something?"

"You just can't trust them."

"So you're saying you can't trust her, huh? I hear you, man." I by no means agreed with his unabashed misogyny, but I was trying to reassure him and reflect what he was saying in a way that did not compromise my own values and beliefs. After several minutes of conversation, he finally calmed down. I looked for the woman and found that she was calm, too, and had the help she needed. My job as a bystander was done.

When emotions aren't running high, you can use Plan B in power-neutral relationships to solve problems, just as an authority figure would do to address challenging behavior. Let's say that you and your spouse are fighting about where to spend the holidays. You want to spend it with your family. Your husband wants to spend it with his. What happens in most cases when conflict like this arises is the couple tries to resolve it by agreeing to a compromise. One year they spend the holidays at one partner's family, the other year they spend it at the other partner's. That arrangement might sound reasonable enough, but it doesn't really satisfy both partners. On any given year, one of the partners will be happy and the other partner will be less so. The arrangement is not a mutually satisfactory solution that addresses *everyone's* concerns. It's *only* a compromise.

In this situation, and in many others that arise in everyday life, compromising is a relatively easy way out, one that leaves both parties feeling somewhat dissatisfied at best. Couples, friends, and others in longer-term relationships tend to use compromises as a way to coast past problems. Once while doing couples counseling, I worked with a married couple who struggled with their sex life. The man wanted more sexual intimacy, and his wife wanted less sex and more emotional intimacy. Classic problem, right? To solve it, the couple created an intricate schedule of when they would have sex, which was not as often as he would've liked but not as infrequent as she would've preferred. That might have tamped down the problem for a period of time, but do you think both spouses felt as if their real concerns had been addressed? Do you think they each felt that the other had taken the time to solicit, acknowledge, and understand the other's concern? It's easy to arrive at compromises, but unless these arrangements reflect an underlying collaborative process, they often don't last as long as we'd like. They also don't allow the parties in the relationship to move to new levels of understanding, respect, and trust.

As this last example suggests, having collaborative Plan B conversations with spouses, friends, and others in your life can prove tricky. In many cases, you might need to broach a topic that seems sensitive. Think through where you might raise this conversation so that it feels nonthreatening. Is it during an evening walk? While you're in the car together commuting home from work? As we've learned in our work with kids, it's important to think about *what* you'll be doing during the conversation. Trying to do Plan B while sitting and staring at each other might make the conversation harder. Talking while your bodies are in motion works far better. As research in neuroscience has demonstrated, patterned, rhythmic, and repetitive motions—walking, riding bikes, hiking, performing chores, even eating—can help regulate your brain stem and open up the cortex so that it can process information better. There's a reason that the military has new recruits march while they learn orders. The marching is soothing and regulating, and it opens the cortex—the smart, reasonable part of our brain.

Also, try to use measured language, taking care not to frame the problem in a way that will arouse an emotional response. If you're a man trying to start a Plan B conversation with his wife about sex, you wouldn't want to kick off the proceedings by making a general statement like "I'm worried about our relationship," as that might cause your wife to feel anxious and overwhelmed. Instead, try to identify some specific difficulties to discuss. For instance: "There seems to be a great deal of tension between us when we're getting ready for bed. There's a sort of elephant in the room about whether we should have sex. Have you noticed that? Why do you think that is?"

When you solicit your partner's concerns, you might uncover information that is hard to hear. For instance, your partner might say, "Well, I still find you attractive and I love having sex, but I just, I don't know, I'm kind of turned off and bored." Your natural response—because you're a human being—is to feel hurt and react defensively. "You're turned off?" you might say. "So you're saying *I'm* boring?" Or you might become fearful about the relationship, thinking that it's doomed. "Oh, great," you say, "so the passion is gone? So now what?" Stop yourself. Remember that any reaction of this nature would bring you out of the state of empathic listening. You would simply be stating your *own* perspective, in emotionally heated terms, instead of listening and absorbing your partner's.

One of the great tragedies of allowing yourself to react is that you'll miss out on a potential trove of valuable information. Instead of reacting to your partner's statement that sex with you is "boring," have her elaborate on that idea by reflecting what you've heard and asking clarifying questions. "You're turned off?" you might ask as a follow-up. "Fill me in. Turned off by what? By me? By what we do in bed?" Of course, this isn't easy to do when you are hearing upsetting information. So hold on tight to the tools used during Plan B's empathy step. Ask questions, take guesses, reflect what you've heard, and provide reassurance. You won't go wrong. You might even discover that the issue isn't what you think. "No, I'm not turned off by you," your partner might say. "I just said I find you attractive. I'm turned off because we always go right to the sex, and I don't feel that we have the kind of emotional intimacy I need."

Now you have another opportunity to learn more. "Okay, so what do you mean by 'go right to the sex'? What would you like to be doing that we're not?"

Perhaps your partner responds that she just wants some more time cuddling or talking or to go out to dinner. So now you're able to clearly recap her concerns: "Okay, if I heard you right, you're saying that you're still interested in me, you still want to have sex, but you're sort of turned off by the way we're having sex and you want to try new things to connect emotionally. Am I hearing you correctly?"

As this is Proactive Plan B, you might take some time before the conversation to anticipate some of the general concerns your partner might raise. That way, if your partner has a hard time thinking about what to say, you can move the discussion forward by hazarding some educated guesses. In this scenario, you might say, "Okay, you're having a hard time expressing your concerns about our sex life. Let me ask you this: Does it have to do with my weight? Is it about how sexy you have been feeling yourself lately?" But don't go much further than that in anticipating your partner's concerns. You don't want to short-circuit the process. The point is to do as much active, open-minded listening as you can.

As with kids, problem solving with adults often doesn't work the first time you try it. Sometimes you must try Plan B multiple times to gain more clarity about the other person's concerns and to tweak the potential solutions. But while Plan B takes work, it's far better than what many couples do in situations like this, and, more generally, what many friends, neighbors, and others in power-neutral relationships do: simply avoid the issue. People in relationships don't talk about what's bothering them because it seems too scary to have a frank conversation. When people do talk, they often make little progress, settling for compromises. Alternately, there is no compromise possible, and endless conflict ensues. Each party lays out his or her desired solution, and the partners battle it out, never reaching a mutually satisfactory solution, and becoming increasingly agitated and upset. The relationship deteriorates. It's far better to talk issues through in a structured way using Plan B. By working together, two people in a power-neutral relationship can generate a solution that feels reasonable, satisfying, and meaningful to everyone.

Plan B: There When You Need It

Linda, a colleague of mine, had been using CPS and Plan B in her work for seven years when she got terrible news: Her father was diagnosed with terminal cancer. He had only months to live. Linda (not her real name) and her siblings had always been close and were used to spending a lot of time together. But tensions existed in the family. After a thirty-year marriage to Linda's mother who passed away, their father had recently gotten re-married to Tracy. Neither Linda nor her three siblings got along well with Tracy. Now that their father was sick, they found themselves fighting with Tracy over numerous issues concerning their father's care and how much access they had to him. "We loved our dad," Linda explained. "Everyone's emotions were super high. We wanted to see our dad more, and Tracy was pushing back against that."

Despite the original prognosis, Linda's father wound up living for another two years before succumbing to his cancer. During this period, it fell to Linda to help negotiate the tensions and try to resolve some of them. As the oldest sibling, she was the rock of the family, or, as she puts it, the family's "pseudoparent." Holiday celebrations took place at her house, and her siblings took their cues from her. Yet playing the parental role here was extremely taxing, because her siblings had trouble seeing their stepmother's point of view as even remotely valid. As Linda reports, she got through this "extremely challenging" period by relying on Plan B.

Linda turned to Plan B on many occasions, including the single hardest moment of her father's illness. He had fallen on a number of occasions, and it became too hard for him to bathe. The siblings decided they just couldn't keep him safe and comfortable at home. Their father had always stated his desire to live at home as long as he could. During the Plan B conversation, held one-on-one with her father, Linda gave him the opportunity to express the concern that led to his desired solution to stay at home. Probing into his thinking, Linda learned that what her father really cared about was maintaining his dignity. She voiced the siblings' concerns: They just couldn't take care of him at home anymore given Tracy's reluctance to involve them, and home hospice care wasn't available in their community. They had kept him there as long as they possibly could, and it was time.

A solution came into focus: If her father cared about his dignity, and the siblings cared about his basic safety and comfort, both concerns could be handled best by transferring him to a hospice facility. As Linda recalls, "Hearing our concerns in that conversation, he could understand better what was necessary. The conversation then became about making his last weeks as enjoyable and meaningful as possible rather than trying to manage risk minute to minute. Dad understood that he would no longer have the dignity he wanted at home. We needed a place that was equipped for it. So we began to talk about how to make this transition to hospice run as smoothly as we could."

The structure of Plan B served Linda as a crutch she could lean on for support. As we've learned by working with kids, the more traumatized someone is, the more they seek out control, structure, and predictability when interacting with others. For those of us who haven't experienced trauma, this need for control carries over when we're dealing with situations that are disturbing or potentially traumatic. With Plan B supporting her, Linda could stay focused during tough conversations and not worry about where they would go, because she knew what the next steps were.

More broadly, the approach allowed Linda to feel more confident and in control throughout the two-year ordeal. No matter what happened to her father, and no matter how her siblings and stepmother reacted, she knew she would be able to handle it. "With Plan B, even if people get stuck in conflict, for instance by being unable to articulate their concerns, you still have a way to move forward. You might not get everything in the first conversation, but you know that you can come back to it. You have the tools you need."

Linda's siblings didn't know about Plan B, but they appreciated it all the same. As their father's illness progressed, they expressed their appreciation to Linda for handling the situation so well. Whenever an issue arose, they called on her to help because "they had a lot of confidence that [she'd] be able to get to the bottom of it." In the wake of their father's death, this pattern has continued. Her sister has even called her to see if she could use CPS to help her husband resolve conflict among members of his team at work.

The more you work with Plan B, and the more you do it in a variety of situations and with a variety of partners, the better you'll get at it. We've seen that kids we work with start to get so proficient at Plan B that they begin applying the approach on their own with parents to solve problems. Adults find that they develop more resourcefulness in problem solving that they can apply throughout their lives, even in extreme situations that might have otherwise overwhelmed them. Put in the time working with CPS in everyday conflict situations, and it will be there for you when you really need it. Instead of feeling overwhelmed by conflict and unsure of what to do, you'll have both the resources and the confidence to push ahead, even when others around you may not.

As time passes, you might even learn how to take Plan B further and use it spontaneously to *prevent* conflicts. When I come home from a business trip, I usually find that my kids have stored up a bunch of requests for me. "Can I do this? Can I get this? Can we go here?" Often when parents are confronted by requests like this, it's tempting to just respond instinctively either yes or no. Yet saying no will often quickly put parents in an Emergency Plan B situation if the child lacks the skills to handle the disappointment (saying yes might lead to the same result if a sibling had pinned his or her hopes on a different course of action). As Plan B has become sort of second nature to me at this point, what I often find myself doing is delaying a decision and instead slipping into the first step of Plan B and asking for information. Even when I'm inclined to bark out a no, I'll say, "I don't know. Fill me in. What's up?"

My kids like this approach, because they understand that my request for information might turn into a yes. They perceive me as taking an open-minded stance, and they're happy because they're given a chance to articulate their points of view. They also know, however, that I might still say no. But they will be heard regardless. The process buys me time as well to think calmly about the issue and understand what's at stake. If after hearing my child's rationale I still have concerns of my own, I can go on to articulate them. Then the two of us can explore options that might address all of our concerns. All along, I also reserve the option of going with Plans A or C, if that's what I want or need after I learn more about the situation.

Most of us don't naturally respond to requests with empathy and collaborative problem solving. Much of the time, we let our emotions determine our responses. It's never easy getting past our emotions, but if you're well practiced in Plan B and collaborative problem solving, you discipline yourself over time to do precisely that. You instinctively respond in a more open-minded way, showing more curiosity about the other person's viewpoint and more objectivity in soliciting it.

We call this approach Spontaneous Plan B. A crisis hasn't arisen yet—emotions have not yet flared up, so there's no need to use Emergency Plan B. You're not using Plan B proactively, either, to address a recurring or predictable problem. Rather, you're using it spontaneously, in the moment, to explore issues before they grow into full-blown conflicts. Spontaneous Plan B is not as easy to perform as Proactive Plan B, because you don't have time beforehand to gather your thoughts or to plan where and when to hold the conversation. It's not as hard as Emergency Plan B, because there is no glaring problem and you don't have to regulate your partner's heightened emotions. In a sense, Spontaneous Plan B is most important for handling everyday life, because it gives you a reliable way to handle myriad issues before they escalate. If you build up to using Spontaneous Plan B, you'll find over time that you're avoiding a lot of conflict. You'll be using Emergency and Proactive Plan B much less often. You and others in your life will still diverge on issues, but you'll have developed a problem-solving rhythm. You'll be communicating much more and finding collaborative solutions, often without even realizing it.

EMERGENCY PLAN B, SPONTANEOUS PLAN B, AND PROACTIVE PLAN B

Emergency Plan B: Solving a problem right in the heat of the moment. Crisis management. De-escalation.[5]

Spontaneous Plan B: Using Plan B in the moment to explore issues that are not yet crises. A way to stay open-minded and prevent issues from mushrooming.

Proactive Plan B: Using Plan B preventatively—*not* in the heat of the moment—to address a recurring or predictable problem.[6]

I'm not suggesting that you apply Spontaneous Plan B to every issue that arises in your life. Some issues are best handled with a quick yes or no. Not every issue has to be discussed. You may find, however, that when you do say yes or no quickly, a certain kind of issue doesn't get resolved well. In the future, you might choose to put off a decision in these instances and move immediately to Spontaneous Plan B. Also, you shouldn't expect to use Spontaneous Plan B until you've put in a lot of practice working with Proactive Plan B. You need to get to the point where you don't even need to think about the steps and how to execute them. Then you'll have a feel for when to use Plan B spontaneously to preempt problems and when not to. Empathy and an eagerness to hear the other person's concerns will begin to flow naturally.

CPS and the Wider World

I often find myself wondering about the effect that individuals adept in CPS might have on the wider world. It's wonderful enough to imagine what our country might be like if a critical mass of staff in our schools, prisons, hospitals, companies, and other institutions practiced Plan B. But what would happen if an entire generation of kids knew how to solve problems collaboratively? For that matter, what would happen if leaders began using CPS and applying the *skill, not will* mind-set in the public sphere to address problems? What if companies and unions used Plan B to resolve or even avoid labor disputes? What if instead of the usual congressional debates, in which candidates battle publicly over different policies, we held public Plan B conversations? What if nations in conflict applied Plan B instead of resorting automatically to Plan A responses, such as the rupturing of diplomatic ties, economic sanctions, and military action?

Take the problem of terrorism—might we use Plan B to address this great scourge of our time? Most politicians espouse Plan A–style responses to the problem of extremism. They talk tough, declaring a war on terror and arguing for cracking down on extremists using military and legal means. Asked during the 2016 presidential election campaign how he would deal with the threat posed by extremist groups, candidate Donald Trump said he would "bomb the shit out of 'em"[7] and broaden the use of torture. While other politicians are less bellicose, they, too, emphasize military solutions, giving much less thought to softer strategies, like engaging preventatively with young people to steer them away from extremist ideology. Confronted with horrible events like the one that happened in my own home-town, the Boston Marathon bombings, our first instincts under-standably are to crack down and rely almost exclusively on our superior power to keep us safe. We also reflexively seek to punish wrongdoers to deter others from becoming extremists or sup-porting their causes. What we don't want to spend much time doing is listening to extremists and understanding their per-spective.

Perhaps we should. Government attempts to crack down have largely failed. In recent years, terrorist acts have become more common, not less. According to terrorism expert Richard Clarke, who famously warned George Bush about an imminent al-Qaeda attack in 2001, there are approximately one hundred thousand terrorists operating today, a substantial increase over the number fifteen years ago. Clarke uses a cancer metaphor to describe the terrorist threat, observing that it has metastasized, becoming more virulent and destructive. The 2015 report of the Global Terrorism Index confirms this, noting that the number of deaths from terrorist attacks increased a staggering 80 percent from 2013 to 2014.[8]

As we've seen, CPS holds that challenging behavior—even that which is immensely violent and destructive—is most accu-rately understood not as a matter of will but as a result of underlying deficits in neurocognitive skills. People who lack skills like flexibility, frustration tolerance, and problem solving unfortunately arrive at terrible solutions to what are usually rea-sonable concerns. This mind-set shift in turn leads us to Plan B as an alternative. Instead of automatically lashing out and pun-ishing, we try under most circumstances to solve problems collaboratively in order to develop and hone underlying skills. The first move we make in applying CPS to extremism is thus to shift our mind-set and show empathy for the perpetrators, interpreting acts of terror as an outgrowth of reasonable concerns met with skills deficits. Separating ourselves from our emotional response to terrorism and its consequences, we dedicate ourselves to understanding as objectively as we can the root, cognitive *causes* underlying terrorist acts.

Let me be clear: *In arguing for empathy, I am not in any way excusing extremist behavior or diminishing the suffering of terrorism's victims.* Acts of violent extremism, big or small, are wrong. They are unacceptable. They are brutal. They are dangerous. And they must be stopped. Period. In thinking about such acts, we must always strive to occupy the victims' perspectives and understand the full trauma inflicted upon them. It's true that we can never truly understand victims' pain and suffering unless we're victims ourselves, but we should try our very best. And yet doing so need not preclude us from also understanding the behavior that produced that trauma. Indeed, if we want to make long-term progress against extremism, and prevent ourselves from occasioning more terrorism unwittingly through our response to it, then we *must* attempt to understand. Why and how did a person become attached to extremist ideology? What takes place in the minds of extremists?

Scholars and terrorism experts have presented a range of explanations for why some people join extremist groups. Some cite identity crises, economic dislocation, or psychological conditions as explanations. Although these factors all possess explanatory power, I would suggest that the most satisfying explanation is a combination of challenges such as these coupled with skills deficits. As I've argued, behind even the vilest, most unacceptable behavior you can almost always find legitimate concerns. Challenging behavior—even that which is extremely violent and callous—occurs because people arrive at completely wrong, unacceptable, and repulsive ways of pursuing their concerns. They lack the skill, not the will, to find better, more socially acceptable ways to obtain their objectives. To respond most productively, we must disavow the violent actions but also seek to grasp the root causes behind them.

So what legitimate concerns motivate people who commit terrorist acts? It may be that they feel alienated or rejected from society. Or their concern might have related to something else entirely—disenchantment with specific government policies, say, or a personal or emotional problem with which they couldn't properly deal. If my clinical work with children is any indication, the nexus of concerns that underlie extremist violence varies among individuals. Behind two actions that appear superficially similar, two very different sets of concerns can lurk.

Whatever these concerns are, we'll never discover them unless we begin asking more questions of extremists. Let's acknowledge the difficulty of this task. For example, one staff member I worked with at a residential treatment center used Plan B to resolve a high-intensity dispute with a teenager. The youth, who had a history of aggressive behavior, had jumped onto a table and was waving a piece of a chair with nails sticking out of it. He told the staff member that he would "bash [her] fucking head in." In that situation, it was immensely challenging for the staff member to see this not as willful aggression but as a result of an underlying skills deficit (and to take steps to empathize with the youth in turn). But she did, and it made all the difference in calming the youth and averting disaster. Terrorist attacks put us *all* in a position similar to the staff member's. We want to lash out against extremists and the people who sympathize with them. But doing so only perpetuates the problem. It fosters even more alienation and anger. By restraining ourselves and connecting with extremists' underlying humanity, we might find ways to defuse negative emotions and steer extremists toward more socially acceptable ways of pursuing their concerns. In the process, we stand to create a more peaceful world.

It might seem novel or even outlandish to think that a collaborative approach could help with behavior as violent, hateful, and destructive as terrorism. Don't we *need* to get tough and wage war on hardened extremists? To some extent, we do. As we've seen with kids, when imminent safety is an immediate concern, it's appropriate to apply Plan A. Likewise, if we know that terrorists are about to strike, we must take decisive action, even if this means disabling or killing the would-be terrorists. We must also pursue an array of other actions to keep populations safe, like dismantling extremist networks, disabling extremist websites and social media accounts, and cracking down on terrorist financing.

But in the absence of an immediate threat, we also have leeway to consider more collaborative solutions to rehabilitate extremists and prevent recruitment of vulnerable youth. As we've seen, CPS works with kids and adults who behave in extreme ways, including those who seem the most irrational or intent on doing harm. Institutions have documented dramatic declines in recidivism among populations that include perpetrators of extreme violence. By uncovering the root causes of challenging behavior and helping us to address those causes, CPS might improve not only traditional prisons, hospitals, and schools but also institutions dedicated to countering violent extremism, such as government-sponsored prevention and rehabilitation programs. We've tried to fight extremism with Plan A without much success. Let's give Plan B a try.

Deploying Plan B in the public arena, whether in relation to extremism or used for any other area of conflict, won't happen on its own. It requires leaders with excellent Plan B skills: leaders who can regulate their own emotions, listen effectively, see past the deadening confines of conventional discipline, understand complex problems, and help generate creative and flexible solutions. In every organization where we've successfully introduced CPS, we did so because we had the firm backing of leaders. In New York City, where our approach was initially controversial, school safety officers eventually embraced CPS because New York Police Department chief Brian Conroy publicly pledged his support. I'll never forget the day he came to one of our training sessions to deliver this message. The hundreds of security officers in the room stood and saluted him in strict military fashion. It was as if the president of the United States had just entered. Conroy walked down the long aisle, took the microphone from my hand, and commanded everyone to be at ease. Then he gave a speech explaining to the officers that the department *expected* them to converse with kids and attempt to empathize with them. He told them that he wanted them to build relationships—not because the department was going soft, but because listening, empathy, and relationship building would get results. It would ease conflict. The department would continue to stand behind officers and protect them, but the officers had to pursue the difficult task of engaging calmly and compassionately with individuals who seemed hostile and bent on antagonizing them.

Anytime violence erupts or political discourse breaks down, you'll find parties in a dispute stuck in their own perspectives, perceiving their solutions as best and regarding solutions advanced by the other parties as inherently flawed. What's missing are the leaders in a political party who would urge us to stop for a moment and listen nonjudgmentally to the other parties' points of view. It's the leaders at every level who would routinely say to the rest of us, "Hmm. I might not like my opponent's solution, but I bet there are reasonable concerns behind it. Let me learn about those concerns and then instead of squabbling over whose solution is better, let's try to put our heads together to reconcile our concerns."

The violent conflict we witness throughout the world owes not simply to the intractability of the disputes involved. It also owes to the persistent Plan A mind-sets of the disputants. Disruptive kids act out because of skill deficiencies, *and* because authority figures impose solutions on them. It's the same with adults in the political arena. A power differential between two individuals causes emotions to flare in the disempowered party. Confronted with someone imposing his will, the subordinate person can act only with more primal, emotional parts of his brain. *Might makes right* leads, in short order, to an inflamed environment where the disempowered are rendered incapable of calmly conversing. When such a disenfranchised person lashes out, a downward spiral of action and reaction follows, and soon both the strong and the weak are locked in their corners, lashing out at one another, and getting nowhere. You see this dynamic playing out today in the thousands of disempowered youth joining extremist groups, the armed uprisings that have engulfed countries from the Middle East to Africa and beyond, the riots that have broken out recently in American cities, and in the rancorous American political scene generally.

Political leaders can pull us all out of this trap by deciding unilaterally to embrace a more productive way of handling conflict. For a leader who has long been locked in conflict with an antagonist, it might seem a radical proposition to put that antagonist on the same level when trying to resolve a problem. Yet it's the only way out, and it might bring us to the kind of pragmatic, collaborative, "hybrid" policy solutions for which the *New York Times* columnist Thomas Friedman has passionately advocated. These are policies that cut across conventional political divides, melding good ideas from opposing sides and bringing disparate parties together in support.[9]

We have so much to gain by listening to one another and engaging collaboratively to resolve our disputes. As we've seen, a structured, empathic, collaborative process helps even the toughest kids to learn new skills and adapt in healthier ways. It would likely help the toughest, most alienated terrorists and political adversaries do so as well. When kids misbehave, it's a question of skill, not will. With disaffected groups of any kind, it's the very same thing.

No More Hurting People

On February 26, 2012, Florida resident George Zimmerman shot and killed Trayvon Martin, an unarmed seventeen-year-old African American youth. In the aftermath of the shooting, a groundswell of young Americans upset about racial disparities in America founded the Black Lives Matter movement. One early activist for this cause, a man named Bobby Constantino, marched from Boston to Florida to protest. During the march, Constantino visited with a second-grade class in Boston that was studying protest and social change. When Constantino suggested that the children and faculty join him for part of the march, a boy named Martin Richard shouted, "Oooh, oooh, oooh, I want to!" in unison with a few budding social activists from among his classmates. Prior to marching, the children made posters showcasing their messages of nonviolence. Martin's read "No more hurting people. Peace."[10]

Tragically, Martin was killed in the 2013 Boston Marathon terrorist attack. After his death, Constantino's photograph of his poster went viral on social media. President Obama also gave it prominent mention in a stirring homage to Boston that he delivered shortly after the bombing. Since then, the image has resurfaced repeatedly on social media and elsewhere as an icon of peace. Following terrorist attacks in 2015 that rattled the city of Paris, Jane Richard, Martin's sister who lost a leg in the bombing, executed a similar image, this time in box letters with vibrant colors and translated into French. Posted to Facebook, it received thousands of likes, shares, and heartfelt emotional responses.[11] During the 2016 presidential election, people in the Twittersphere affixed the hashtag #NoMoreHurtingPeoplePeace to critiques of Donald Trump's divisive language and to express sadness and exasperation following other mass shootings and acts of terror.

Martin's story suggests not merely the importance of peace and compassion but also the surprising power of kids to lead the rest of us. As Martin's parents have suggested, "Kids are natural bridge builders—on the playground, at the lunch table, in the classroom—and all of their simple acts of kindness can add up to make a big difference."[12] This book has also argued that kids are bridge builders. The world's most challenging kids can help us uncover the pervasive and devastating failings of conventional discipline. They can help us understand the true causes of challenging behavior, and they can help us grasp better, more compassionate ways of resolving conflict wherever we experience it. Learning from challenging kids, and incorporating the findings of the latest science, we can make our society safer, more humane, and more prosperous.

But transcending both traditional discipline and hierarchical ways of interacting means surmounting a critical challenge, one that may be articulated implicitly by Martin's famous poster. No more hurting people—that means *all* people, including those whose behavior seems most irritating, hurtful, obnoxious, or obscene. Like crime, delinquency, and other social ills, conventional discipline and its "get tough" ethic also hurts people. If getting tough kept the rest of us safer over the long term, we might perhaps judge the harm done a necessary price to pay for our collective well-being. But most of the time, getting tough doesn't keep us safer. By any measure, it's an abysmal failure. To achieve more peace, we must build more bridges, not just with people we like but with people who seem to wish to do us harm.

Seem to wish—that's the key. When you analyze it, people who commit crimes, act out in school, or rage against their parents almost never do it out of malicious intent. They do it because they don't know another way. And that's because they struggle with problem-solving skills. Attending to these skills can help these people behave in more productive, adaptive ways. So let's honor the memory of victims like Martin Richard, and secure the future of the next generation of children growing up today by opening our minds and our hearts to people with whom we're in conflict. In the spirit of Martin Richard, let's invite these people in—for their sake as well as our own. Like the thousands of parents, teachers, school safety officers, and hospital staff who've deployed CPS, we'll be amazed at what we can accomplish.

Epilogue

Twelve year-old Adam (not his real name) had one of the worst trauma histories I'd ever seen. As a toddler, he witnessed his mother being abused by his biological father, and, afterward, by her boyfriend. His biological parents and his mother's boyfriend neglected him, abused him emotionally, tied him up with duct tape and handcuffs, hit him in the head with a bottle, and locked him up in a room for long periods. Although his caseworkers didn't know for sure, they suspected that Adam had also been sexually abused.

As you would expect, this intense, unremitting trauma devastated Adam. As he grew older, he behaved disruptively and acted out violently against others and himself. When he was still in elementary school, he was placed in a foster home, but his foster parents couldn't control him, so the state put him in another foster home, and then another. He was hospitalized. And then hospitalized again. Eventually, he landed in a special residential treatment facility for extremely challenging kids. This was the end of the line for Adam, other than jail eventually. There were no other treatment options available for kids like him. While at this facility, he destroyed property, hit and kicked other people, hurt himself by banging his head against the wall and choking himself, and threatened to commit suicide. Psychologists diagnosed him with a number of disorders, including oppositional defiant disorder and attention deficit hyperactivity disorder. The staff who dealt with him on a daily basis described him as haunted and tortured. He flew into rages several times a day and had to be physically restrained multiple times a month.

By the time I learned about Adam, staff at his residential facility had given him medications, a range of traditional therapies, and the neurofeedback therapy described in chapter 7. They had also begun practicing Plan B with him. His behavior had improved somewhat since he'd started Plan B, but he had a long way to go. He had become so fearful and distrustful of authority figures, and of people in general, that it was hard for him to solve problems collaboratively, even with well-meaning staff. One of the skill areas with which he struggled most had to do with cognitive inflexibility, or black-and-white thinking. When life didn't go as he expected, he lost it, throwing violent tantrums. That made a lot of sense: His life had been so chaotic for so long that to the extent he could, he was trying to regain some sense of control. But as we've seen, neuroscience has another, more satisfying explanation. All the chronic stress he'd experienced had likely delayed his brain development.

Sometime after Adam had started working with CPS, I had a chance to see a video of him participating in a Plan B conversation.

Adam had wanted to go barefoot because he felt more comfortable that way. Staff members were concerned that he'd step on something sharp or pick up an infection. Adam got so upset when staff wouldn't let him go barefoot that he had to be physically restrained. So a staff member had called him in to try to resolve the issue. In the video, Adam appears intimidated and extremely dysregulated to be sitting face-to-face with an authority figure. It's subtle: On the surface, he seems calm. Look closely, though, and you see that his mouth and hands are twitching, and that he's bouncing his leg repeatedly. This poor kid who has been through so much, and is so distrustful of adults, is scared out of his wits and jumping out of his skin.

When the staff member asks Adam about his concerns, he learns that Adam wants to go barefoot simply because he feels uncomfortable wearing socks. The staff member articulates his concerns about the safety and hygiene implications of walking around barefoot. Then the staff member starts the process of generating solutions. But he is new to Plan B, so he makes a misstep. Instead of asking Adam what he thinks they might do to address both of their concerns, he says, "So what do you think we can do to make you feel more comfortable wearing socks?" Without realizing it, the staff member has veered back toward imposing his own desired solution—forcing Adam to wear socks. In that moment, he was doing Plan A masquerading as Plan B.

Oh, crap, I thought to myself as I heard the staff member's question. There we were, trying to do some solid therapeutic work with Adam. We were trying to help him develop new, healthier, more trusting relationships with authority figures. We were *so close* in this conversation to making progress—and this

staff member slipped up. Adam would come away from this conversation *distrusting* authority figures more. He would learn that
even this apparently nice and caring staff member would listen to
his concern but then still try to impose his will. In his eyes, this
staff member would look pretty similar to so many other adults
in his life who had told him what to do and then harshly punished him when he didn't comply. Adam's struggles would continue. His behavior would only get worse.

Happily, that's not what happened. Watching the video, I
was surprised to see that Adam is nonplussed by the staff member's question. Rather than respond to it directly, giving in to the
staff member's implicit demand that he wear socks, he answers *as
if* the staff member has invited him to collaborate to address both
of their concerns, and has not tried to impose his own solution.
"Well," Adam says, "you could get me some slippers." It's a beau-
tiful moment. This kid, who was quite familiar with Plan B, is
telling the staff member, "Hey, look, what you just said, that's
actually Plan A. Let me give you a solution that would work for
both of us."

Through past Plan B conversations, Adam had internalized
the notion that during the problem-solving process he could express his concerns and authority figures really would listen to
him. So that when an authority figure wasn't quite listening to
him the way he should have been during a Plan B conversation,
Adam was able to recognize that and steer the conversation back
toward collaborative problem solving.

I feel so much heartache working with challenging kids.
Their stories are devastatingly tragic. But in a fleeting moment
like this, I can perceive all the difference that Plan B makes. New

pathways have been created in Adam's traumatized brain. Trust has been formed. New, more productive relationships with authority figures have taken root. Yes, Adam will need many more moments like this to recover from what he's endured. He'll need years of collaborative problem solving, and likely other therapies. He might never heal entirely. And yet hope lives on. Think of it: An adult wants to force a terribly traumatized kid to wear socks, but the kid isn't lashing out. Instead, he contributes an idea that might work for everyone. A creative solution. One that *he* thought of. Slippers.

Acknowledgments

First and foremost, I want to thank the people without whom this book would not exist—the children, adolescents, and adults with whom I have had the privilege to work over the years. Some have described them, or at least their behavior, as challenging. Personally, I'm glad they've challenged us. They've challenged us to rethink our approach to discipline, pushed us to think and behave in more humane, compassionate, and understanding ways, and showed us that every person is able to change. I'm grateful to them for doing so.

I am similarly indebted to the scores of parents and colleagues alongside whom I've had the pleasure of learning. I often say I've had the easy job—traveling around teaching people a new way of helping others to change. Those I've taught have the hard work day in, day out—whether in homes, classrooms, offices, treatment centers, or correctional facilities. You hear from some of them in the stories I tell throughout the book, but there are too many to possibly include. But you know who you are, and I hope you know how much I appreciate and respect your inspiring work.

Closer to home, the support of the leaders of the Psychiatry Department at Massachusetts General Hospital (MGH), specifically my mentor, Dr. Jerrold Rosenbaum, and Joy Rosen has been invaluable and means so much to me. You find out who your friends are when the chips are down, and I will never forget that. And of course a huge thank-you to my colleagues at Think:Kids at MGH, for the work you do each and every day to help spread our approach around the world. Like me, you believe in the philosophy behind our approach and are on a mission to make sure it becomes the new conventional wisdom.

I would also like to acknowledge the mentorship of my former partner, Dr. Ross Greene, who has done so much to help children and families with behavioral challenges. I learned a tremendous amount from you; for that I will always be grateful.

It does take a village to write a book like this, and I would like to thank the very talented Seth Schulman, who dove head-first into this project and has been a remarkable collaborator; my editor, Marian Lizzi, and her team at Penguin Random House for believing in the promise of this book and working so hard to get it right; and my agent, Lorin Rees, for the idea in the first place! Thank you to any co-collaborators I might not have mentioned by name as well. Together we have made quite a team.

Finally, thank you to my family. You have shared this journey with me. Thanks, Kim, for free advice from a professional writer. Thanks, Brooke, for always being there for me in so many ways. Thank you, Christina, for all you've done for so many years to raise our three amazing kids together while allowing me to do this work. Jack, Carter, and Paige: thanks for making us look like great parents! You are each incredible in your own, completely unique ways, and I am so proud to call myself your dad. Thanks, Mom and Dad and Grandma and Grandpa, for being models of unconditional love and understanding through thick and thin and thick again, and for showing me how important it is to listen to children and take their perspectives seriously.

Notes

Introduction

1   *Oregon State Hospital: Significant Actions Taken to Improve Safety and Promote Patient Recovery, but Further Improvements Are Possible*, Secretary of State Audit Report, September 9, 2015, accessed April 3, 2017, https://oregonaudits.org/2015/09/09/oregon -state-hospital-significant-actions-taken-to-improve-safety -and-promote-patient-recovery-but-further-improvements-are -possible/.

2   Internal, unpublished data compiled from the Oregon State Hospital.

3   M. R. Durose, A. D. Cooper, and H. N. Snyder, *Recidivism of Prisoners Released in 30 States in 2005: Patterns from 2005 to 2010*, Bureau of Justice Statistics Special Report, April 2014, NCJ 244205.

4   C. R. Reynolds et al., "Are Zero Tolerance Policies Effective in the Schools? An Evidentiary Review and Recommendations," *American Psychologist* 63 (2008).

5   C. Porath, *Mostering Civility: A Manifesto For the Workplace* (New York: Grand Central Publishing, 2016).

6   R. W. Greene, *The Explosive Child: A New Approach for Understanding and Parenting Easily Frustrated, "Chronically Inflexible" Children* (New York: HarperCollins, 1998).

7   B. D. Perry, "The Neurosequential Model of Therapeutics: Applying Principles of Neuroscience to Clinical Work with Traumatized and Maltreated Children," in *Working with Traumatized Youth in Child Welfare*, ed. Nancy Boyd Webb (New York: Guilford Press, 2006).

8   D. H. Pink, *Drive: The Surprising Truth About What Motivates Us* (New York: Riverhead Books, 2009); R. M. Ryan and E. L. Deci, "Intrinsic and Extrinsic Motivations: Classic Definitions and New Directions," *Contemporary Educational Psychology* 25 (2000); R. M. Ryan and E. L. Deci, "Self-determination Theory and the Facilitation of Intrinsic Motivation, Social Development, and Well-being," *American Psychologist* 55 (2000).

9   C. Dweck, *Mindset: The New Psychology of Success* (New York: Random House, 2006).

10   A. Duckworth, *Grit: The Power of Passion and Perseverance* (New York: Scribner, 2016).

Chapter One: Skill, Not Will

1   Ryan and Deci, "Self-determination Theory and the Facilitation of Intrinsic Motivation, Social Development, and Well-being."

2   U.S. Department of Education, Office for Civil Rights, Civil Rights Data Collection, *Data Snapshot: School Discipline*, Issue

Brief no. 1, March 2014, accessed April 3, 2017, http://ocrdata
.ed.gov/Downloads/CRDC-School-Discipline-Snapshot.pdf;
New York Civil Liberties Union, "New City Suspension Data
Shows Suspensions Are Down but Racial Disparities Persist,"
October 31, 2016, accessed March 8, 2017, from https://www
.nyclu.org/en/press-releases/new-city-suspension-data-shows
-suspensions-are-down-racial-disparities-persist.

3   W. K. Mohr, A. Marin, et al., "Beyond Point and Level Systems:
Moving Toward Child-Centered Programming," *American
Journal of Orthopsychiatry* 79 (2009).

4   B. F. Skinner, *The Behavior of Organisms: An Experimental Analysis*
(New York: Appleton-Century-Crofts, 1938); D. L. Gilbert and
D. M. Wegner, "B. F. Skinner: The Role of Reinforcement and
Punishment," in *Psychology* (New York: Worth, 2011).

5   K. A. Dodge, J. E. Lochman, J. D. Harnish, J. E. Bates, and
G. S. Pettit, "Reactive and Proactive Aggression in School
Children and Psychiatrically Impaired Chronically Assaultive
Youth," *Journal of Abnormal Psychology* 106 (1997): 37–51;
D. A. Waschbusch, and M. T. Willoughby, "Criterion Validity
and the Utility of Reactive and Proactive Aggression: Com-
parisons to Attention Deficit Hyperactivity Disorder, Oppositional Defiant Disorder, Conduct Disorder, and Other Measures
of Functioning, *Journal of Clinical Child Psychology* 27, no. 4
(1998).

6   Dr. Greene is founding director of the nonprofit organization
Lives in the Balance and a faculty member at Virgina Tech. He
is the author of *The Explosive Child*, among other books.

7   S. Crandall Hart and J. C. DiPerna, "Teacher Beliefs and Responses Toward Student Misbehavior: Influence of Cognitive Skill Deficits," *Journal of Applied School Psychology* 33, no. 1 (2017): 1–15, doi: 10.1080/15377903.2016.1229705.

Chapter Two: The Science Behind Challenging Behavior

1   D. Wechsler et al., *Wechsler Intelligence Scale for Children*, 4th ed. (WISC-IV) (Texas: Pearson, 2003).

2   G. A. Miller, "The Magical Number Seven, Plus or Minus Two: Some Limits on Our Capacity for Processing Information," *Psychological Review* 101 (1955).

3   E. Strauss, E. Sherman, and O. Spreen, *A Compendium of Neuropsychological Tests: Administration, Norms, and Commentary* (Oxford: Oxford University Press, 2006); E. Kaplan et al., *Boston Naming Test* (Philadelphia: Lea & Febiger, 1983).

4   C. Hughes et al., "Trick or Treat? Patterns of Cognitive Performance and Executive Function Among 'Hard to Manage' Preschoolers," *Journal of Child Psychology and Psychiatry* 39 (1988).

5   D. Schultz, C. Izard, and G. Bear, "Children's Emotion Processing: Relations to Emotionality and Aggression," *Development and Psychopathology* 16 (2004).

6   See, for instance, E. Willcutt, E. Sonuga-Barke, J. Nigg, and J. Sergeant, "Recent Developments in Neuropsychological

Models of Childhood Psychiatric Disorders," in *Biological Child Psychiatry* (Basel, Switzerland: Karger Publishers, 2008), 195–226; J. Stieben, M. D. Lewis, I. Granic, P. D. Zelazo, S. Segalowitz, and D. Pepler, "Neurophysiological Mechanisms of Emotion Regulation for Subtypes of Externalizing Children," *Development and Psychopathology* 19, no. 2 (2007): 455–80; S. H. Van Goozen, P. T. Cohen-Kettenis, H. Snoek, W. Matthys, H. Swaab-Barneveld, and H. Van Engeland, "Executive Functioning in Children: A Comparison of Hospitalised ODD and ODD/ADHD Children and Normal Controls," *Journal of Child Psychology and Psychiatry* 45, no. 2 (2004): 284–92; K. A. Dodge, J. E. Lansford, V. S. Burks, J. E. Bates, G. S. Pettit, R. Fontaine, and J. M. Price, "Peer Rejection and Social Information-Processing Factors in the Development of Aggressive Behavior Problems in Children," *Child Development* 74, no. 2 (2003): 374–93.

7   J. Biederman et al., "Impact of Adversity on Functioning and Comorbidity in Children with Attention-deficit Hyperactivity Disorder," *Journal of the American Academy of Child and Adolescent Psychiatry* 34 (1995).

8   E. Willcutt, E. Sonuga-Barke, J. Nigg, and J. Sergeant, "Recent Developments in Neuropsychological Models of Childhood Psychiatric Disorders," in *Biological Child Psychiatry* (Basel, Switzerland: Karger Publishers, 2008), 195–226.

9   On the link between language difficulties and challenging behavior, see, for instance, A. P. Kaiser, X. Cai, T. B. Hancock, and E. M. Foster, "Teacher-Reported Behavior Problems and

Language Delays in Boys and Girls Enrolled in Head Start," *Behavioral Disorders* 28, no. 1 (2002): 23–39; Z. Y. Zadeh, N. Im-Bolter, and N. J. Cohen, "Social Cognition and Externalizing Psychopathology: An Investigation of the Mediating Role of Language," *Journal of Abnormal Child Psychology* 35, no. 2 (2007): 141–52.

10 Language in this paragraph was drawn from R. W. Greene and J. S. Ablon, *Treating Explosive Kids: The Collaborative Problem-Solving Approach* (New York: Guilford Press, 2005); R. W. Greene et al., "Psychiatric Comorbidity, Family Dysfunction, and Social Impairment in Referred Youth with Oppositional Defiant Disorder," *American Journal of Psychiatry* 159 (2002).

11 E. M. Hallowell and J. J. Ratey, *Driven to Distraction: Recognizing and Coping with Attention Deficit Disorder from Childhood Through Adulthood* (New York: Pantheon, 1994).

12 Research linking poor working memory skills to challenging behavior includes M. J. Endres, M. E. Rickert, T. Bogg, J. Lucas, and P. R. Finn, "Externalizing Psychopathology and Behavioral Disinhibition: Working Memory Mediates Signal Discriminability and Reinforcement Moderates Response Bias in Approach-Avoidance Learning," *Journal of Abnormal Psychology* 120, no. 2 (2011): 336. Other research linking executive functioning skills weaknesses to challenging behavior includes A. B. Morgan and S. O. Lilienfeld, "A Meta-analytic Review of the Relation Between Antisocial Behavior and Neuropsychological Measures of Executive Function," *Clinical Psychology Review* 20, no. 1 (2000): 113–36; K. Schoemaker, H. Mulder, M. Deković, and W. Matthys, "Executive Functions in

Preschool Children with Externalizing Behavior Problems: A Meta-analysis," *Journal of Abnormal Child Psychology* 41, no. 3 (2013): 457–71.

13   C. S. Kranowitz, *The Out-of-Sync Child: Recognizing and Coping with Sensory Processing Disorder* (New York: TarcherPerigee, 2006).

14   Research linking problems with self-regulation to challenging behavior includes S. Ciairano, L. Visu-Petra, and M. Settanni, "Executive Inhibitory Control and Cooperative Behavior During Early School Years: A Follow-up Study," *Journal of Abnormal Child Psychology* 35, no. 3 (2007): 335–45; M. Brophy, E. Taylor, and C. Hughes, "To Go or Not to Go: Inhibitory Control in 'Hard to Manage' Children," *Infant and Child Development* 11, no. 2 (2002): 125–40; M. A. Raaijmakers, D. P. Smidts, J. A. Sergeant, G. H. Maassen, J. A. Posthumus, H. Van Engeland, and W. Matthys, "Executive Functions in Preschool Children with Aggressive Behavior: Impairments in Inhibitory Control," *Journal of Abnormal Child Psychology* 36, no. 7 (2008): 1097–1107; K. C. Brocki, L. Eninger, L. B. Thorell, and G. Bohlin, "Interrelations Between Executive Function and Symptoms of Hyperactivity/Impulsivity and Inattention in Preschoolers: A Two Year Longitudinal Study," *Journal of Abnormal Child Psychology* 38, no. 2 (2010): 163–71.

15   A. L. Hill, K. A. Degnan, S. D. Calkins, and S. P. Keane, "Profiles of Externalizing Behavior Problems for Boys and Girls Across Preschool: The Roles of Emotion Regulation and Inattention," *Developmental Psychology* 42, no. 5 (2006): 913;

R. W. Greene and A. E. Doyle, "Toward a Transactional Conceptualization of Oppositional Defiant Disorder: Implications for Assessment and Treatment," *Clinical Child and Family Psychology Review* 2, no. 3 (1999): 129–48; J. Stieben, M. D. Lewis, I. Granic, P. D. Zelazo, S. Segalowitz, and D. Pepler, "Neurophysiological Mechanisms of Emotion Regulation for Subtypes of Externalizing Children," *Development and Psychopathology* 19, no. 2 (2007): 455–80.

16   S. H. Van Goozen, P. T. Cohen-Kettenis, H. Snoek, W. Matthys, H. Swaab-Barneveld, and H. Van Engeland, "Executive Functioning in Children: A Comparison of Hospitalised ODD and ODD/ADHD Children and Normal Controls," *Journal of Child Psychology and Psychiatry* 45, no. 2 (2004): 284–92; M. L. Ellis, B. Weiss, and J. E. Lochman, "Executive Functions in Children: Associations with Aggressive Behavior and Appraisal Processing," *Journal of Abnormal Child Psychology* 37, no. 7 (2009): 945–56.

17   Greene and Ablon, *Treating Explosive Kids*.

18   K. A. Dodge, J. E. Lansford, V. S. Burks, J. E. Bates, G. S. Pettit, R. Fontaine, and J. M. Price, "Peer Rejection and Social Information-Processing Factors in the Development of Aggressive Behavior Problems in Children," *Child Development* 74, no. 2 (2003): 374–93.

19   Research linking weakness in social thinking skills with challenging behavior includes M. J. Chandler, S. Greenspan, and C. Barenboim, "Assessment and Training of Role-Taking and Referential Communication Skills in Institutionalized Emo-

tionally Disturbed Children," *Developmental Psychology* 10, no. 4 (1974): 546; J. C. Gibbs, G. B. Potter, A. Q. Barriga, and A. K. Liau, "Developing the Helping Skills and Prosocial Motivation of Aggressive Adolescents in Peer Group Programs," *Aggression and Violent Behavior* 1, no. 3 (1996): 283–305; J. D. Coie and K. A. Dodge, "Aggression and Antisocial Behavior" in W. Damon and N. Eisenberg, eds., *Handbook of Child Psychology* (1998): 779–862; E. T. Cook, M. T. Greenberg, and C. A. Kusche, "The Relations Between Emotional Understanding, Intellectual Functioning, and Disruptive Behavior Problems in Elementary-School-Aged Children," *Journal of Abnormal Child Psychology* 22, no. 2 (1994): 205–19; D. Schultz, C. E. Izard, and G. Bear, "Children's Emotion Processing: Relations to Emotionality and Aggression," *Development and Psychopathology* 16, no. 2 (2004): 371–88; K. A. Dodge, J. E. Lansford, V. S. Burks, J. E. Bates, G. S. Pettit, R. Fontaine, and J. M. Price, "Peer Rejection and Social Information-Processing Factors in the Development of Aggressive Behavior Problems in Children," *Child Development* 74, no. 2 (2003): 374–93; K. L. Bierman, and J. A. Welsh, "Assessing Social Dysfunction: The Contributions of Laboratory and Performance-Based Measures," *Journal of Clinical Child Psychology* 29, no. 4 (2000): 526–39.

20   B. D. Perry, "The Neurosequential Model of Therapeutics: Applying Principles of Neuroscience to Clinical Work with Traumatized and Maltreated Children," in *Working with Traumatized Youth in Child Welfare*, ed. Nancy Boyd Webb (New York: Guilford Press, 2006).

21   S. J. Lupien et al., "Effects of Stress Throughout the Lifespan on the Brain, Behaviour and Cognition," *Nature Reviews Neuroscience* 10 (2009).

22   B. Perry and M. Szalavitz, *Born for Love: Why Empathy Is Essential and Endangered* (New York: Morrow, 2011); B. Perry and M. Szalavitz, *The Boy Who Was Raised as a Dog* (New York: Basic Books, 2006).

23   B. Perry, "Maltreatment and the Developing Child: How Early Childhood Experience Shapes Child and Culture," The Margaret McCain Lecture Series, September 23, 2004, accessed April 3, 2017, http://www.lfcc.on.ca/mccain/perry.pdf.

24   V. J. Felitti, R. F. Anda, D. Nordenberg, et al., "Relationship of Childhood Abuse and Household Dysfunction to Many of the Leading Causes of Death in Adults: The Adverse Childhood Experiences (ACEs) Study," *American Journal of Preventive Medicine* 14 (1998): 245–58.

25   R. W. Greene, J. S. Ablon, and J. C. Goring, "A Transactional Model of Oppositional Behavior: Underpinnings of the Collaborative Problem Solving Approach," *Journal of Psychosomatic Research* 55 (2003).

26   C. S. Dweck, *Mindset: The New Psychology of Success* (New York: Ballantine Books, 2006).

Chapter Three: Discipline Gone Awry

1   L. Tolstoy, *Anna Karenina*, trans. David Magarshack (New York: New American Library, 1961).

2   W. S. Gilliam and G. Shahar, "Preschool and Child Care Expulsion and Suspension: Rates and Predictors in One State," *Infants and Young Children* 19, no. 3 (2006): 228–45.

3   In New York City, for instance, the number of suspensions increased from 49,588 in 2006 to 69,643 in 2012 *(Keeping Kids in School and Out of Court, Report and Recommendations*, New York City School–Justice Partnership Task Force, May 2013, accessed April 3, 2017, https://www.nycourts.gov/IP/justice -forchildren/PDF/NYC-School-JusticeTaskForceReport AndRecommendations.pdf).

4   R. J. Skiba et al., "Consistent Removal: Contributions of School Discipline to the School-Prison Pipeline" (paper presented at the School to Prison Pipeline Conference: Harvard Civil Rights Project, Boston, May 16–17, 2003). According to one analysis, for instance, "As the rate of school suspension increases, average achievement scores in math, reading, and writing decline." See "Are Zero Tolerance Policies Effective in the Schools? An Evidentiary Review and Recommendations," *American Psychologist* 63, no. 9 (2008): 852–62.

5   G. J. Boyle et al., "A Structural Model of the Dimensions of Teacher Stress," *British Journal of Educational Psychology* 65 (1995); M. H. Abel and J. Sewell, "Stress and Burnout in Rural and Urban Secondary School Teachers," *Journal of Educational Research* 92 (1999).

6   Abel and Sewell, "Stress and Burnout in Rural and Urban Secondary School Teachers."

7   Telephone interview with Sam Leuken, January 15, 2016.

8 Jill Bloomberg, unpublished letter to the author, January 21, 2014.

9 J. Chan, J. LeBel, and L. Webber, "The Dollars and Sense of Restraints and Seclusion," *Journal of Law and Medicine* 20, no. 1 (2012): 73–81. At one facility in the United States, "restraint use claimed more than 23% of staff time and $1.446 million in staff-related costs which represented nearly 40% of the operating budget for the inpatient service." In a study of psychiatric units in the UK, an estimated 50 percent of "all nursing resources were expended to manage conflict and implement containment procedures," https://www.researchgate.net/publication/233534086_The _dollars_and_sense_of_restraints_and_seclusion.

10 A. R. Pollastri et al., "Minimizing Seclusion and Restraint in Youth Residential and Day Treatment Through Site-Wide Implementation of Collaborative Problem Solving," *Residential Treatment for Children & Youth* 33 (2016).

11 J. LeBei and R. Goldstein, "The Economic Cost of Using Restraint and the Value Added by Restraint Reduction or Elimination," *Psychiatric Services* 56 (2005).

12 According to a study conducted in thirty U.S. states. Please see: "State of Recidivism: The Revolving Door of America's Prisons," Pew Center on the States, April 2011, pp. 1–2, http:// www.pewtrusts.org/m/media/legacy/uploadedfiles/pcs_as sests/2011/pewstateofrecidivism.pdf.

13 D. Barrett, "Prison Firm CCA Seeks to Reduce Number of Repeat Offenders," *Wall Street Journal*, updated September 12,

2014, accessed April 3, 2017, http://www.wsj.com/articles /prison-firm-cca-seeks-to-reduce-number-of-repeat -offenders-1410561176.

14   M. Santora, "City's Annual Cost Per Inmate Is $168,000, Study Finds," *New York Times*, August 23, 2013, accessed April 3, 2017, http://www.nytimes.com/2013/08/24/nyregion/citys -annual-cost-per-inmate-is-nearly-168000-study-says.html.

15   C. Porath and C. Pearson, "The Price of Incivility," *Harvard Business Review*, January–February 2013, accessed April 3, 2017, https://hbr.org/2013/01/the-price-of-incivility.

16   Ibid.

17   HBS Working Knowledge, "Workplace Stress Responsible for Up to $190B in Annual U.S. Healthcare Costs," *Forbes*, January 26, 2015, accessed April 3, 2017, https://www.forbes.com /sites/hbsworkingknowledge/2015/01/26/workplace-stress -responsible-for-up-to-190-billion-in-annual-u-s-heathcare -costs/2/#4c97f48f3957.

18   C. M. Pearson and C. L. Porath, *The Cost of Bad Behavior: How Incivility Is Damaging Your Business and What to Do About It* (New York: Portfolio, 2009).

Chapter Four: Plan B

1   Greene, *The Explosive Child*; Greene and Ablon, *Treating Explosive Kids*.

2   Ibid.

3   Ibid.

4   Greene, *The Explosive Child*.

5   Ibid.

6   Ibid.

7   B. D. Perry, "The Neurosequential Model of Therapeutics: Applying Principles of Neuroscience to Clinical Work with Traumatized and Maltreated Children," in *Working with Traumatized Youth in Child Welfare*, ed. Nancy Boyd Webb (New York: Guilford Press, 2006).

8   B. D. Perry and J. S. Ablon, Through the Prism Conference presentation, Medford, Oregon, 2014.

9   M. Hone, "Collaborative Problem Solving as a Unifying Approach: Program and Organizational Implementation from a Multi-Service Children's Mental Health Agency," Children's Mental Health Organization Conference, November 24, 2014, at the Marriott Toronto Downtown Eaton Centre.

10   Perry, "The Neurosequential Model of Therapeutics: Applying Principles of Neuroscience to Clinical Work with Traumatized and Maltreated Children."

11   G. Heath et al., "Investigating Mechanisms of Change in the Collaborative Problem Solving Model" (submitted manuscript).

12   Greene, *The Explosive Child*; Greene and Ablon, *Treating Explosive Kids*.

Chapter Five: Parenting 2.0

1   R. W. Greene et al., "Effectiveness of Collaborative Problem Solving in Affectively Dysregulated Children with Oppositional Defiant Disorder: Initial Findings," *Journal of Consulting and Clinical Psychology* 72 (2004).

2   M. Johnson et al., "Attention-deficit/Hyperactivity Disorder with Oppositional Defiant Disorder in Swedish Children—an Open Study of Collaborative Problem Solving," *Acta Paediatr* 101 (2012).

3   T. Epstein and J. Saltzman-Benaiah, "Parenting Children with Disruptive Behaviours: Evaluation of a Collaborative Problem Solving Pilot Program," *Journal of Clinical Psychology Practice* 1, no. 1 (2010): 27–40.

4   Unpublished New York Police Department data.

5   Pollastri et al., "The Collaborative Problem Solving Approach: Outcomes Across Settings," *Harvard Review of Psychiatry* 21 (2013).

6   A. Martin, H. Krieg, F. Esposito, D. Stubbe, and L. Cardona, "Reduction of Restraint and Seclusion Through Collaborative Problem Solving: A Five-Year Prospective Inpatient Study," *Psychiatric Services* 59, no. 12 (2008): 1406–12.

7   Pollastri et al., "The Collaborative Problem Solving Approach.

8   E. Ercole-Fricke et al., "Effects of a Collaborative Problem Solving Approach on an Inpatient Adolescent Psychiatric Unit," *Journal of Child and Adolescent Psychiatric Nursing* 29 (2016).

9   Pollastri et al., "The Collaborative Problem Solving Approach.

10   F. Fuchs Schachter and R. K. Stone, "Difficult Sibling, Easy Sibling: Temperament and the Within-Family Environment," *Child Development* 56, no. 5 (1985): 1335–44.

11   J. Johnston, "The Ghost of the Schizophrenogenic Mother," *Virtual Mentor* 15 (2013), accessed October 20, 2016, http://journalofethics.ama-assn.org/2013/09/oped1-1309.html.

12   E. L. Deci, R. Koestner, and R. M. Ryan "A Meta-analytic Review of Experiments Examining the Effects of Extrinsic Rewards on Intrinsic Motivation," *Psychological Bulletin* 125 (1999): 627. See also S. Davie, "Should You Reward Your Child for A Grades?" accessed April 3, 2017, http://www.rochester.edu/news/pdfs/RichTSTb.pdf.

Chapter Six: Transforming Workplaces

1   *Workplace Conflict and How Businesses Can Harness It to Thrive*, CPP Global Human Capital Report, July 2008, accessed April 3, 2017, http://img.en25.com/Web/CPP/Conflict_report.pdf.

2   For a discussion of how unresolved conflict damages workplace morale and the bottom line in Canada, see B. Howatt, "The Long-term Costs of Not Resolving Workplace Conflict," *Globe and Mail*, July 16, 2015, accessed October 3, 2016, http://www.theglobeandmail.com/report-on-business/careers/leadership-lab/the-long-term-costs-of-not-resolving-workplace-conflict/article25527147/. Celebrity chef Anthony Bourdain

has credited open communication and the airing of grievances with creating a functioning, happy, and extremely loyal workforce in the chaotic restaurant business. See G. Morse, "Management by Fire: A Conversation with Chef Anthony Bourdain," *Harvard Business Review*, July 2002, accessed October 3, 2016, https://hbr.org/2002/07/management-by-fire-a-conversation-with-chef-anthony-bourdain.

3 L. Solomon, "Two-Thirds of Managers Are Uncomfortable Communicating with Employees," *Harvard Business Review*, March 9, 2016, accessed October 3, 2016, https://hbr.org/2016/03/two-thirds-of-managers-are-uncomfortable-communicating-with-employees.

4 For an alternative approach, please see S. Bernstein and S. Ablon, "Collaborative Problem Solving: An Effective Approach for Managing Conflict in the Workplace," Mediate.com, August 2011, accessed April 3, 2017, http://www.mediate.com/articles/BernsteinS1.cfm.

5 E. J. Wilson III et al., "Empathy Is Still Lacking in the Leaders Who Need It Most," *Harvard Business Review*, September 21, 2015, accessed October 3, 2016, https://hbr.org/2015/09/empathy-is-still-lacking-in-the-leaders-who-need-it-most.

6 P. Korkki, "Conflict at Work? Empathy Can Smooth Ruffled Feathers," *New York Times*, October 8, 2016, accessed April 3, 2017, https://www.nytimes.com/2016/10/09/jobs/conflict-at-work-empathy-can-smooth-ruffled-feathers.html?_r=0.

7   D. Goleman, *Emotional Intelligence: Why It Can Matter More Than IQ* (New York: Bantam Books, 1995).

8   A. Mckee, "How to Hire for Emotional Intelligence," *Harvard Business Review*, February 5, 2016, accessed April 3, 2017, https://hbr.org/2016/02/how-to-hire-for-emotional-intelligence; %20https://hbr.org/2015/04/how-to-look-for-emotional -intelligence-on-your-team.

9   Stanford psychologist Carol Dweck introduced and popularized the idea of a growth mind-set in her bestselling book *Mindset* (2006). The philosophy also gained currency when Silicon Valley start-up ClassDojo partnered with educational specialists at Stanford to teach kids about the importance of a growth mind-set (by unveiling a digital monster named Mojo). Their growth mind-set programming was so successful that the company teamed up with Harvard specialists to create related programming on empathy. See J. Anderson, "Meet Mojo, the Monster Stanford and Harvard Are Using to Teach Your Kids 'Growth Mindset' and Empathy," *Quartz*, September 27, 2016, accessed October 3, 2016, http://qz.com/791388/meet-mojo-a -monster-stanford-helped-create-to-teach-your-kids-that -effort-matters-more-than-iq/).

10   That such emotions can linger beneath the surface was evident in 2016 when news broke of one of the biggest scandals in banking history. Employees at Wells Fargo created millions of artificial accounts to meet staggeringly high sales quotas. When thousands were fired for corruption, disgruntled employees took to Reddit, narrating how they were pressured into this

dishonest practice because they feared they would fail to make their bonuses or provide for their families. Employees describe feeling threatened and coerced into acquiescing to this unlawful behavior (called "cross-selling"). Those who expressed moral qualms were usually fired for not meeting their quotas. See M. Corkery and S. Cowley, "Wells Fargo Warned Workers Against Sham Accounts, but 'They Needed a Paycheck,'" *New York Times*, September 16, 2016, accessed October 3, 2016, http://www.nytimes.com/2016/09/17/business/dealbook /wells-fargo-warned-workers-against-fake-accounts-but -they-needed-a-paycheck.html?_r=0; A. Beltz, "Inside Wells Fargo, Front-Line Employees Describe Immense Pressure, Few Rewards," *Star Tribune*, September 24, 2016, accessed October 3, 2016, http://www.startribune.com/inside-wells -fargo-front-line-employees-describe-immense-pressure-few -rewards/394694611/.

11   This section and other portions of this chapter draw heavily from Bernstein and Ablon, "Collaborative Problem Solving: An Effective Approach for Managing Conflict in the Workplace."

12   R. A. Heifetz, *Leadership Without Easy Answers* (Cambridge, MA: Belknap Press of Harvard University Press, 1994).

13   Quoted in C. Thomason, "Brainstorming Doesn't Work—Four Exercises to Flex Your Creativity," *Guardian*, September 12, 2016, accessed October 3, 2016, https://www.theguardian .com/small-business-network/2016/sep/12/brainstorming -doesnt-work-four-exercises-flex-creativity.

14   A. Robb, "Why Men Are Prone to Interrupting Women," *New York Times*, March 19, 2015, accessed October 3, 2016, http://nytlive.nytimes.com/womenintheworld/2015/03/19/google-chief-blasted-for-repeatedly-interrupting-female-government-official/.

15   See E. Harrell, "The Solution to the Skills Gap Could Already Be Inside Your Company," *Harvard Business Review*, September 27, 2016, accessed October 3, 2016, https://hbr.org/2016/09/the-solution-to-the-skills-gap-could-already-be-inside-your-company; J. Donovan and C. Benko, "AT&T's Talent Overhaul," *Harvard Business Review*, October 2016, accessed October 3, 2016, https://hbr.org/2016/10/atts-talent-overhaul.

16   See Heifetz, *Leadership Without Easy Answers*.

17   A. R. Pollastri, L. Wang, P. J. Vuijk, E. N. Hill, B. A. Lee, A. Samkavitz, E. B. Braaten, J. S. Ablon, and A. E. Doyle, "The Thinking Skills Inventory: A Brief Screening Tool to Assess Neurocognitive Skill Deficits Relevant for Treatment of Youth Behavioral Challenges" (submitted manuscript).

18   Dr. B. Perry, Think:Kids webinar, October 21, 2016.

19   K. Reynolds Lewis, "Dear Customer Service Centers, Please Stop It with the Scripted Empathy," *Fortune*, March 23, 2016, accessed April 3, 2017, http://fortune.com/2016/03/23/call-scripted-empathy/.

20   T. Drollinger, L. B. Comer, P. T. Warrington, "Development and Validation of the Active Empathetic Listening Scale," *Psychology & Marketing* 23 (2006).

Chapter Seven: Getting Along Better in Daily Life

1   Pollastri et al. "The Thinking Skills Inventory: A Brief Screening Tool to Assess Neurocognitive Skill Deficits Relevant for Treatment of Youth Behavioral Challenges."

2   Neither of these are their real names, and I've also changed other identifying details for their protection.

3   For example, see E. Vandewater and J. E. Lansford, "Influences of Family Structure and Parental Conflict on Children's Well-being," *Family Relations* 47 (October 1998): 323, DOJ 10.2307 /585263.

    J. B. Kelly, "Children's Adjustment in Conflicted Marriage and Divorce: A Decade Review of Research," *Journal of the American Academy of Child & Adolescent Psychiatry* no. 39, 8: 963–73.

4   Dr. L. Miller, "Hostage Negotiations: Psychological Strategies for Resolving Crises," *PoliceOne*, May 22, 2007, accessed August 22, 2016, https://www.policeone.com/standoff/articles /1247470-Hostage-negotiations-Psychological-strategies-for -resolving-crises/.

5   Greene, *The Explosive Child*.

6   Ibid.

7   P. Engel, "Donald Trump: I Would Bomb the Sh– Out of ISIS," *Business Insider*, November, 13, 2015, http://www.busi nessinsider.com/donald-trump-bomb-isis-2015-11.

8   Institute for Economics and Peace, "Global Terrorism Index, 2015," (November 2015): 2.

9   T. Friedman, "Beware: Exploding Politics," *New York Times*, March 2, 2016, accessed April 3, 2017, http://www.nytimes.com/2016/03/02/opinion/beware-exploding-politics.html.

10   E. Randall, "The Story Behind Martin Richard's Peace Sign," *Boston Magazine*, April 30, 2013, accessed September 14, 2016, http://www.bostonmagazine.com/news/blog/2013/04/30/the-story-behind-martin-richards-peace-sign/.

11   Jennifer Hansler, "Boston Bombing Victim Shares Message Parisians Understand," ABC News, November 18, 2015, accessed January 11, 2018, http://abenews.go.com/US/boston-bombing-victim-shares-message-parisians-understand/story?id=35282317.

12   B. Richard and D. Richard, "Martin Richard's Parents: The Power of 'No More Hurting People, Peace,'" *Time*, September 14, 2015, http://time.com/4021594/martin-richard-bridge-builder-campaign.

Index

INDEX

About the Author

J. STUART ABLON, PHD, is a clinical psychologist who specializes in understanding and helping children, adolescents, and adults with challenging behavior. Dr. Ablon is the Director of Think:Kids in the Department of Psychiatry at Massachusetts General Hospital. He is also Associate Professor and the Thomas G. Stemberg Endowed Chair in Child and Adolescent Psychiatry at Harvard Medical School. Dr. Ablon teaches parents, educators, clinicians, managers, and leaders, and consults with schools, treatment programs, and other organizations throughout the world in the Collaborative Problem Solving approach. Dr. Ablon lives in the Boston area with his family. He is the proud parent of three children.

6-18

NB